THE MAN
WHO SANK
THE
TITANIC ?

THE LIFE
AND TIMES
OF
CAPTAIN
EDWARD J. SMITH

GARY COOPER

Witan Books

Gary James Cooper was born in 1965 and spent the first few years of his life in Hanley, Stoke-on-Trent, before his family moved to the nearby village of Bucknall. Educated at Hanley High School, he subsequently worked as a typewriter mechanic and an illustrator before returning to full-time education in 1988. He gained a B.A. (Hons.) in English and Modern Studies in 1991 and an M.A. in Victorian Studies in 1994. Gary currently works as a presentations assistant at the Gladstone Pottery Museum in Stoke-on-Trent and this is his first book.

Witan Creations
1998 Main Catalogue

WTN 001   "Butcher's Tale/Annie, With The Dancing Eyes" –The Witan (animal rights protest single), 1981 - £1.85 + 55p. p & p.

WTN 002   "The Rise And Fall Of Rock" – Jeff Kent (484 page critical Rock music history, 56 photographs), 1983 - £5.75 + £1.75 p & p.

WTN 008   "I Have Survived The Witan Experience" badges (printed green on white), 1985 - 25p. + 30p. p & p.

WTN 024   "Port Vale Forever" – Jeff Kent (10 track first ever football club album, with songbook), 1992 – £5 including p & p.

WTN 025   "The Port Vale Record 1879-1993" – Jeff Kent (292 page statistical compilation, 60 photographs), 1993 – £14.25 including p & p.

WTN 027   "The Mercia Manifesto: A Blueprint For The Future Inspired By The Past" – The Mercia Movement (128 page radical political manifesto), 1997 – £7.80 including p & p.

THE MAN WHO SANK THE TITANIC ?

THE LIFE AND TIMES OF CAPTAIN EDWARD J. SMITH

First published in November 1992 by Witan Books.

Second (revised) edition published in September 1998 by Witan Books, Cherry Tree House, 8 Nelson Crescent, Cotes Heath, via Stafford, ST21 6ST, England. Tel: (01782) 791673.

WTN 028

ISBN 0 9529152 2 7

A CIP record for this book is available from the British Library.

Cover concept: Jeff Kent.
Cover artwork and design: Alicia Brown.
Editors: Rosalind Kent and Jeff Kent.
Typeset, printed and bound by: PKA Print & Design, Dunning Street, Tunstall, Stoke-on-Trent, ST6 5AP. Tel: (01782) 575280.

To my parents

WILLIAM JAMES COOPER
&
BARBARA COOPER

ACKNOWLEDGEMENTS

The author and publisher would like to express their thanks to the following for their invaluable assistance in the production of this book:
Rosalind Kent, Allan Staples, Ken Longmore, Pete Henaghan, Alicia Brown, Peter Pearce, Roger Simmons, Paris, Smith and Randall, Cyril Kent, Alan Downs, Stoke-on-Trent City Central Reference Library and staff, Lisa Verity/the National Maritime Museum, Martin Phillips/University of Keele Library, G. W. Robinson, Geoffrey Dunster R.D., R.N.R., Lt. Commander Raymond J. Davies R.D., R.N.R, the Cooper family for their support throughout and last but not least, Biddie Garvin, who gave the author the idea for this book in 1987.

ILLUSTRATION CREDITS

Illustrations were kindly supplied by the following:
Gary Cooper – front cover right, back cover, 2-5, 7, 10-13, 27, 31, 51, 53, 54, 59-62, 69; The Warrilow Collection, University of Keele Library – front cover left, 25; Roger Simmons – 8, 17, 20, 32, 38, 63, 67; John P. Eaton and Charles A. Haas – 41, 48, 50, 66, 68; "Daily Sketch" – 37, 45, 52; "White Star Magazine" – 9, 15; "Illustrated London News" – 19, 49; "Daily Mirror" – 39, 46; Father Francis M. Browne Collection, Society of Jesus – 40, 44; Mariners Museum, Newport News – 14; State Library of New South Wales – 18; Ken Marschall/Rustie Brown Collection – 22; Empire State Notables – 30; Harland and Wolff Ltd. – 35; Mr. and Mrs. George A. Fenwick – 55; "Washington Evening Star" – 57; National Archives, Washington – 64; Staffordshire Sentinel Newspapers Limited – 70.

Contents

Prologue

Dominating Beacon Park, Lichfield, is a statue now green with age, but which is still an impressive sight. The figure's bronze arms are folded and his face surveys the shrubbery with an air of command. On the plaque these words are stamped:

'Commander Edward John Smith, R.D., R.N.R. Born January 27th, 1850, died April 15th, 1912, bequeathing to his country the memory and example of a great heart, a brave life and heroic death. "Be British." '

The casual passer-by could be forgiven for thinking that he was looking at the statue of some worthy of Lichfield, but there he would be wrong. Commander Smith was no native of the city, perhaps he had never been there in his entire life, and the unveiling of his statue there in 1914 caused widespread anger in Lichfield because of that. His home town was Hanley, the principal town of the Potteries, the federation of six towns that today form the city of Stoke-on-Trent, which was then too embarrassed to acknowledge the memory of this remarkable but ill-fated man because of his connection with one of the greatest disasters in maritime history. On 14th April 1912, the newest, largest, most luxurious ocean liner in the world was on its maiden voyage from Southampton to New York. At 11.40 p.m., the ship struck an iceberg in mid-Atlantic and, despite being considered 'unsinkable', at 2.20 a.m. on 15th April, she nose-dived to the ocean floor taking over 1,500 people with her. The ship was named Titanic; her captain was named Edward John Smith.

This is his story –

Prologue

1

Early Days In The Potteries

The world knows the area by its pottery: Stoke-on-Trent, the Potteries, "the Five Towns" are the several names it goes under. Beyond its borders, the popular image of the city is one of dirty rows of Victorian terraces and a skyline dominated by the ubiquitous "bottle ovens", the distinctively shaped pottery kilns that belched out thick, acrid black smoke both night and day. That, of course, is how it used to be, certainly during the nineteenth century and the earlier part of this century, but today Stoke-on-Trent is very different. Gone are the bottle ovens, except for a few museum pieces, while the Clean Air Act has allowed the locals to see what colour the sky should be. But, as our story begins in the middle of the nineteenth century, it is proper to go back to that popular image.

To some the Potteries was a filthy place of cobbled streets and plain rows of houses caked with soot, inhabited by low, guttural peasants who spoke with some kind of hacking brogue. To others, like one of its famous sons, novelist Arnold Bennett, it was a place filled with real people, genuine characters, who were poor but tough and extremely proud, though they generally despaired of their surroundings. To Bennett, the Potteries oozed the very tales of existence that the novelist was hard put to site elsewhere. To visitors to the area, such as Bennett's close friend H.G. Wells, it was the forsaken cityscape that left an impression; the Dante's inferno of the ovens at night stayed with Wells as an image full of ethereal beauty and horror, so potent that it found its way into his "War of the Worlds", as a way of describing the spectacle of the destruction caused by the Martian war machines.

Such a city of brick and fire seems, therefore, the last place on earth that anyone would look for a future sea captain, but so it was.

1

EARLY DAYS IN THE POTTERIES

On Sunday 27th January 1850, Edward John Smith, the son of Edward and Catherine Smith, was born at the family home of 51 Well Street, in Hanley.

Both Hanley and Well Street can bear a little description in so far as they relate to the Smith family. If ever a town was built for landlubbers it was Hanley in the nineteenth century, linked to the outside world by a few roads, a single railway line and a couple of canals. Like that of most of the Potteries towns the population was generally introspective, their energies given over to the burgeoning pottery industry. Yet Hanley was not so heavily devoted to ceramic manufacture as the other towns and then as now was the the main shopping and business area of the region – not for nothing did Arnold Bennett point to Hanley (the town of his birth) as the 'Chicago of the Five Towns'.

The town had started life in about the thirteenth century as a vill comprising three virgates of land, held in 1212 A.D. by one William of Hanley. Actually, this comprised two villages, Upper and Lower Green (the latter was also known as Hanley Green), and it is around the latter that the modern marketplace has formed. For many centuries, the village did not expand overmuch, but following the construction of the Trent and Mersey Canal and the Wedgwood works at Etruria, the population and influence of Hanley exploded. The modern layout of the town still follows the pattern of the eighteenth century village with its winding town centre and 'archipelago of island sites', as one recent history described it. The more recent additions to the town came with the early decades of the nineteenth century – its imposing civic buildings, the former large indoor market (on the site of which the modern Potteries Shopping Centre is now built) and more importantly as far as this story is concerned, the large Wellington housing estate that came to form the south-east edge of Hanley and effectively doubled the size of the town. Constructed in the main on an eastward-facing slope of land, the Wellington estate was edged to the rest of the town by Charles Street and Well Street, which were the first to be constructed.

Many of the later streets that formed the estate drew their titles from the names of individuals or events associated with the

Napoleonic Wars – Wellington Road, Waterloo Road, Nelson Place, Picton Street and Eagle Street, but Well Street was so named for a far more parochial reason, namely it was the site of (or was at least near) two wells. One of these was the Woodwall Well, which was a spring with a pump attached from which water carts run by "higglers" filled up. The Woodwall Well was the main source of water for the entire town and was frequented by one particular old higgler, who then drove his cart around the town selling the water for ½d. a bucketful. In the early years of the nineteenth century, piped water was a rarity and generally of an inferior quality to this springwater, so the Woodwall Well and other nearby springs were still in use in the 1840s and they seem to have carried on (even though the supply of water had grown limited due to the flow being diverted on many of its hidden streams) until about 1850.

As one of the first streets in the new estate, Well Street was constructed towards the very peak of the bank, which gave the place an advantage as the wind and rain could scour away the debris and sewage that accumulated in the back alleys. The street was paved with cobbles and "quarries", and the two-up, two-down, high-fronted terraced houses marched step-like two-by-two down the bank. The street itself still exists in part and in name. In the 1960s, the upper part of the street was demolished to make way for a series of maisonettes and blocks of flats, while more recently, modern houses have replaced the terraces on one side of what remains of Well Street. The remains also survived the 1980s, having been narrowly missed by the large modern bypass known as the Potteries Way, the construction of which destroyed several of the nearby old streets. But, on one side of Well Street still exists a row of tall, Victorian terraced houses that run from number 51, where Smith was born, down to the Rising Sun pub built in 1884. With its shrubs and trees, a green, a small children's playground and on a sunny day a fine view over distant Berry Hill, it does not seem to be a bad street in which to live: a far cry from the smoke-stained, low rent working-class accommodation of mid-Victorian Britain.

On 30th March 1851, when the census was taken, there were four people living at 51 Well Street. The head of the household was Edward Smith, a 46-year old potter who had been born in Hanley in about 1805. His wife Catherine was 42 and worked as a grocer. She had been born Catherine Marsh either in Stoke-upon-Trent or Penkhull in about 1809. In 1831 she had married a potter named George John Hancock, in Wolstanton, by whom she had had two children, Joseph and Thirza. After being widowed she had met and married Edward Smith, also in Wolstanton, in 1847. Joseph had been born in Penkhull in about 1833, but he was no longer at home; he had joined the merchant navy and was making steady progress in his chosen career. Thirza, the daughter, was, however, still living with her mother and in 1851 was 15 years old and working as a milliner and dressmaker. The census claims that she was born in Tunstall, though it seems she was actually born in Wolstanton on 1st January 1836 and was baptised at the Tunstall Primitive Methodist Chapel on 17th January. Oddly, the records also show the baptism of the similarly named Thirra Hancock, daughter of John and Catherine Hancock, in Wolstanton on 7th January that year.

Edward John, the first and only child of Edward and Catherine Smith, was the fourth family member entered on the census form that year; he was one year old.

There is no available record of his baptism, but other information shows that the family were Primitive Methodists by faith, while young Ted later found himself educated within the confines of mainstream Wesleyan Methodism. One of the main problems with any biography of Edward John Smith is that there are precious few views of the man himself and his youth and upbringing are particularly deficient in that respect. However, religion and education promote certain characteristics in people, so a study of his background can give us a few hints as to how he thought and the kind of life he led.

Primitive Methodism, a Nonconformist faith, was a splinter faction of Wesleyan Methodism advocated by the radical Hugh Bourne and his followers, who in 1811 were expelled from mainstream Methodist circles because of their fiery and feverish style of worship. The Primitives still believed in the strong Methodist doctrines of hymnody, worship and temperance, but whereas Wesleyan Methodism found its mainstay of support in the

4

middle-classes, the Primitives appealed to the workers in those areas where heavy industry had taken a hold. Their laymen preachers could often be seen in the first half of the nineteenth century haranguing crowds of working-class men and women from a street corner or from the back of a cart. So stylised was their performance that they earned the nickname "Ranters" and the dislike of the Victorian establishment. However, unlike many of their modern evangelistic counterparts, they were dedicated to their cause. Theirs was a partial throwback to seventeenth century Puritanism and they believed powerfully in what has become known as the Protestant Work Ethic, that men could earn salvation through hard work rather than unwavering piety, a factor that struck home powerfully with the working masses. Not surprisingly, from its formation Primitive Methodism grew in popularity in the industrial centres of England. By 1850, the Primitives were receiving particularly strong support in the Potteries, as well as in northern mining towns and in remote East Anglian villages.

In the early 1850s, however, the Smith family began to outgrow its working-class and Primitive Methodist background, when in either late 1851, or in 1852, Edward Smith gave up working as a potter and, moving to 17 Well Street, a property owned by one Elizabeth Smith and comprising a 'house, shop and yard', he set himself up as a grocer. He is listed as a 'Shop-keeper' in the 1852-1853 edition of "Slater's Commercial Directory" and appears as such in successive editions of "Kelly's Directory" for many years after. The business was successful and within a few years, Edward Smith either bought the property from its former landlady, or inherited it, because Elizabeth Smith may have been his mother. From then on Edward ran the store with his wife and increased the family fortune to such a degree that Catherine eventually became the leaseholder on several nearby Well Street properties. Young Ted therefore received a good education because of his family's increased fortunes and status. Most of the stories later written about Captain Smith describe him as having been 'a potter's son from Hanley', and at the time of his birth his father was a potter, but from his infancy upwards, Ted (whom one school friend, as we shall see, regarded as 'respectable') grew up as a grocer's son, a member of the respectable middle-classes.

He was educated at the Etruria British School, the premises of which were situated at the back of the Wesleyan Chapel (which still exists) in Lord Street, Etruria, not far from the large Wedgwood pottery factory around which the town of Etruria was built. The school rooms were later given over to the Sunday school, while the regular day pupils were absorbed by the Etruria Board School that took over in 1881. As the school itself was situated within the confines of the Wesleyan Chapel, it was there that young Ted was imbued with the strong Methodist traits that many later noted in him.

The British School had been one of a number of embryonic places of education supported by the wealthy Wedgwood family, some of whose children were educated at the school. The school was some distance from Well Street, a fact that seems to have led to the speculation that the Smith family went to live in Etruria, though this most certainly was not the case. The British School had a reputation for sound teaching and embraced the Methodist doctrines that the Smiths obviously wanted their child to inherit. It was probably for these reasons that young Ted was enrolled there as an infant pupil. The school was not free of charge (compulsory free education began in 1890) and the Smith family may have had to pay something like the three shillings a month that the school charged in 1862, when it became a part of the Etruria Unsectarian School.

Prior to 1861 and the creation of the school boards, education in general was kept afloat through individual charity and the aid of volunteers. The British School was lucky in that its patrons were the wealthy Wedgwood family who could afford to employ good teachers. As headmaster of their school, the Wedgwoods employed Alfred Smith, a native of Derbyshire, who seems to have been a forbearing and highly respected teacher by the standards of the time. Certainly, many if not most of the school's old boys later held him in high esteem. Only a few years after Ted left his school, Alfred Smith was appointed as the first secretary to the Hanley School Board, whilst he also spent time teaching future luminaries such as Jesse Shirley and Cecil Wedgwood as private pupils. In later life, many of the old boys (Ted included) attended a reunion in his honour. Alfred Smith died at the age of 78 in 1911, but that was still half a lifetime away from the teacher at the Etruria British School. According to Joseph Turner, a fellow pupil and close friend of Ted, Alfred Smith taught the boys under his charge a simple creed – love of 'God, Queen and Country', and occasionally found time to break free of the strictures of the Lancaster system of education to regale the boys with tales of brave British deeds, one of which will be gone into later. But first it is perhaps a good idea to have a look at a typical day in a mid-Victorian school and to meet some of the people who knew Captain Smith as a boy.

British Schools were what were called monitorial schools, which were ones where the responsibility for a great deal of the teaching was delegated down a chain of pupil monitors from one teacher. The schools of this type were usually subdivided by religious faith; the Anglican community was catered for by the National Schools, while the Nonconformists sent their children to the British Schools. These schools employed the Bell or Lancaster systems of tuition respectively. Both were systems (arrived at separately) whereby a very limited number of teachers could hand over the lessons to the monitor who would see that the large classes each got the same amount of tuition per pupil. Both systems demanded heavy regimentation of the schoolchildren, because only in this way, as Lancaster's spelling book said, could 500 children 'be taught from 1 book instead of 500'. Simply put, the Lancaster method of education was a variation on the theme of learning by rote, a process of copy, learn and don't question that modern teachers would have nightmares about. Such a system offered no room for self-expression and had built into it the obvious faults that any children not able to understand the lessons were left behind and the benefits to the whole class were lost if the monitors themselves were not well educated.

A typical day in such a school went something like this:

School would start at 9 a.m. for all classes (there were classes for boys, girls and infants in separate classrooms). Before the lessons began, the school said the morning prayer before the monitor general (usually a senior pupil) called out all the lesser monitors and asked for a head count of each class. Considering that Ted Smith was to spend the majority of his adult working life in a job where a hierarchical chain of command governed his existence, such a roll call was to become very familiar.

After the head count, on command the children sat down on bare wooden benches (they were lucky if they had desks to work on) and waited for a series of orders: 'Clean slates', 'Show slates clean', 'Lay down slates', 'Hands down'. All this was done with noisy bustle. The monitor general, who had received his or her orders from the teacher or headmaster, then gave out the letters or phrases to be copied and these were written either on a blackboard or on a card which was held up before the whole class, who then copied it out on their own small slates. When they were all done, the monitor general called out, 'Hands down. Show slates,' and the monitors then did the round checking for any mistakes before further orders of 'Lay down slates', 'Clean slates', 'Show slates clean' were issued. Then a fresh set of words and phrases were set out and it started all over again. It was very cheap and was all dependent on the ability of individual monitors. During the years that Ted was at school, though, this system was receiving a great deal of criticism and the slightly more efficient one of having a group of paid pupil teachers may have been in use.

The mornings were generally given over to writing and reading, usually in that order, and after the spelling lessons, groups of children were brought out to read from the board or a child would come in with a card bearing the alphabet and the class would say out loud each letter as it was called out. The children were also tested on their ability to count to 100 accurately.

At about 10.30, there was a five-minute break before they returned to their lessons. These carried on until about 11 a.m., when the class had to study their catechism or religious induction, so important to the Victorian sense of religion: the Creed, the Lord's Prayer, the Ten Commandments and a few scattered psalms, all learnt and taught in the same manner as the alphabet. After that was done, the class said grace "before meat" and at noon went home.

They returned at about 2 p.m., said grace "after meat" and then got back to the lessons. For the youngest pupils, the afternoon was spent in the same manner as the morning, but as the scholars got older the afternoons were given over increasingly to arithmetic, tables and accounts. At 4.30, more prayers were said, followed perhaps by evening hymns. Then, finally, the children were allowed to go home.

In many schools, all of this was done with strict regularity and all too often with levels of discipline that today would be tantamount to sadism. Piety was rigorously enforced and the child was indoctrinated to 'know his place', 'respect his betters' and a host of other homilies the Victorians dreamed up to control their children. Of course it is only possible to speculate how close all this was to the routine Ted knew at school, as the system did vary, but that the school did operate along these lines is perhaps borne out by the fact that Ted numbered among his closest friends boys that quite often were many years his junior, so if he had taken up the duties of a class monitor, he would have had occasion to meet many of them from day to day. For instance, there was Edmund Jones who knew him as a 'senior boy' at the school and considered him to be 'a quiet, respectable, courageous lad who never put himself to the front too much'. Jones also recalled that Ted was always on hand to defend the weaker and younger boys if anyone ever fell to bullying them, essentially acting like a big brother. Spencer Till, the son of an Etruscan grocer who was to remain lifelong friends with Ted, was seven or eight years his junior.

Another boy, Joseph Turner, who was mentioned earlier, was two years younger than Ted. He, though, remembered him in a rather different light as a high-spirited boy and at first the two of them were enemies. Fights broke out whenever they got on one another's nerves and after one such playground scuffle the two angry young boys were collared by the headmaster, Alfred Smith, who told them that if they had to fight, to do so after school, not during it. So they did, after the lessons had ended for the day and before either boy went home. Joe Turner, seconded by Herbert Greatbach, and Ted, seconded by Joe's brother Edward, went to the nearby Hall Fields adjoining the Wedgwood home of Etruria Hall to continue the struggle. They went at each other with swordsticks in what by modern standards seems a very formalised way of having a scrap. After the fight had gone on for a short time, Joe got in a lucky strike and caught Ted a stinging blow on the neck. This infuriated Ted so much that in a red rage he rushed at Joe, put down his guard and thrashed him until he howled. However, as with most schoolboy quarrels, one good fight to vent their feelings seems to have made things better and in time they grew to be great friends.

Life at school for the boys did have its lighter moments. On warm summer days, as Cecil Wedgwood later recalled, it was not uncommon to find 'boatloads' of schoolboys from the British School taking a canal trip by barge down to the Wedgwood factory and perhaps in the process the boys were wont to belt out a few songs in an age where you made your own entertainment. Spencer Till certainly seemed to remember school songs as part and parcel of his youth.

Of course when the boys were back at school, Alfred Smith would tell them tales of the sea. Joe Turner recalled with some irony in later life that he had listened with fascination to Alfred Smith's rendering of the wreck of the Birkenhead, which was a ship whose fate was often later compared and contrasted with that of the Titanic.

The Birkenhead was a war steamer carrying 630 people on their way to Algoa Bay, South Africa, 132 being crewmen and the rest being detachments of the 12th, 74th and 91st infantry regiments, plus the soldiers' wives and children. One night in February 1852, off the aptly named Danger Point on the African coast, the vessel struck a reef of submerged rocks at speed and became a hopeless wreck, rapidly shipping water. Lieutenant-Colonel Seton, the most senior army officer present, called the other officers together and impressed on them the need to maintain order, before placing himself and his men at the disposal of the ship's skipper. Sixty men were assigned to the pumps, while others looked to the lifeboats or threw the unfortunate horses overboard to lighten the ship. What few boats remained undamaged were loaded with the women and children. Almost immediately as the last boat pulled away, the ship split, crosswise, and the stern where most of the men were gathered began to sink. The captain then ordered the men to abandon ship and to swim for the boats, but Seton and his officers, seeing that such an action would swamp the already crowded boats, ordered their men into ranks and asked them to remain there. And they did so, officers and men, veteran soldiers and the newest of recruits – the greater majority of them all stood waiting for the end. In moments the sea engulfed the Birkenhead and the men, some sinking, some swimming or clinging to wreckage, could be seen from the boats. After the ship had finally gone down, only a few survivors were picked up – the rest were drowned or taken by prowling sharks. Of the 630 men, women and children aboard the Birkenhead, only 192 survived.

It was an incredible story of self-sacrifice that became enshrined in seagoing folklore as the origin of the 'women and children first' maxim that sailors and male passengers were expected to live up to should they ever be unlucky enough to be involved in a shipwreck. It is more than likely that Ted Smith heard his teacher recite this tale or heard it later during his many years at sea, or even from his elder half-brother, Joseph Hancock, who had risen rapidly through the ranks of the merchant navy.

By 1861, a great deal had happened to the Smith family. For a start, Thirza had got married to an engineer named William Harrington and by then they had a house of their own at 18 Well Street, just across the road from the Smiths' grocer's store. There, Edward and Catherine had extra mouths to feed, two-year old George J. Hancock, no doubt the son of Joseph Hancock who must have been away at sea, and a 22-year old niece of Edward, whose first name was Ellen, but whose surname and occupation are unreadable on the census return. Ted's age on this return is wrongly given as ten years; he was in fact eleven years old and about to enter his last year at school.

When Ted left school at the age of twelve, he gained employment at the Etruria Forge (also known as the Etruria Furnaces), a large metal smelting and pressing concern that was later incorporated into the Shelton Bar steel works. The forge was fairly near to his old school, being situated on the bank of the Trent and Mersey Canal just to the west of the Wedgwood pottery. The manager of the forge at that time was the grandfather of Edmund Jones, who had known Ted at school. Ted may have done a number of jobs during his time at the forge, but eventually he became the operator of the huge Nasmyth steam hammer, a monstrous contraption constructed like a giant letter "Y" turned on its head, which was used for the shaping of the largest of wrought iron components with mighty blows of its hydraulic hammer, but according to its maker, James Nasmyth, it was a machine so well engineered that with a skilled operator the hammer could hold an egg without breaking it. Ted's job fascinated Joe Turner, who one night stayed away from home to sit with him through his night shift in the little box that accommodated the driver.

Early in 1865, there was a strike in the iron industry due to wage cuts caused by a fall off in the iron trade and a resulting drop in prices for the metal. Overall, the industry became depressed and it may have been because of the gloom caused by the strike, coupled perhaps with sea stories told to him by his half-brother, Joseph, that made Ted consider a career at sea. But, whatever the cause, early in 1867 he gave up his job at Etruria Forge and, accompanied by a group of friends, one of whom was Joe Turner, Ted went to Liverpool to meet Joseph Hancock who was by then the captain of an American sailing ship called the Senator Weber (or Senator Webber). It seems from the available evidence that Ted went to Liverpool with every intention of enlisting in the mercantile marine, rather than in his excitement joining up on the spur of the moment, as one romantic story would have us believe. This is borne out by the tale related by Joe Turner, who was actually the one who got excited and tried to join up there and then, but Captain Hancock refused to take him because he had neither an outfit, nor his parents' consent, a statement which seems to imply that Ted had one or both of them. Crestfallen, Joe and the others returned to the Potteries. Ted, though, was signed aboard the Senator Weber and taken onto the books of her owners, Messrs. Andrew Gibson and Co. of Liverpool. The date was 5th February 1867, when Ted Smith gave up his life as a landlubber and began his long and remarkable career at sea.

2

Sail and Steam

'In old days going to sea was a sort of last resort. The lot of the apprentice serving his four year term, usually on a sailing ship, was almost intolerably hard and only the toughest constitutions were able to survive it.'

So ran one job description (c.1928) of what life was like for those drawn to the merchant service. In the 1860's and until only recently, there were just two avenues open to achieving a certificate as an officer: by apprenticeship, or by promotion from the ranks. Most followed an apprenticeship, serving the four-year indenture indicated above. This could be reduced to three years if the candidate completed two years aboard one of the approved training ships prior to gaining his first sea berth. Once aboard ship, the training then concentrated more on turning the apprentice into a sailor rather than an officer. Most of the working day for the average apprentice was, therefore, spent labouring with the deckhands on the many onerous maintenance tasks to be done around the ship. Some unscrupulous shipping companies used the apprentices solely as a source of cheap labour, but more reputable lines attached the apprentices to one of the mates, under whose tutelage they might learn something of their duties.

It has formerly been assumed that Ted Smith started his career at sea as just such an apprentice, but this no longer appears to be the case. Indeed, if his own account is to be trusted, Ted seems to have taken the second route outlined above, that of promotion from the decks, signing aboard the Senator Weber as an ordinary sailor. He then passed from ship to ship, gaining the "sea time" he needed to apply for a certificate. Against this is the fact that only a very few men ever made the leap from the deckhand ranks to that of officer. However, all the available evidence does seem to indicate that Ted was one of these exceptions. On his "Application to be Examined for a Certificate of Competency" for second mate, in the section headed "List of Testimonials and Statement of Service from First Going to Sea", he is shown progressing from boy to able seaman. Apprentices stayed as such during the entire term of their indentures as they were never promoted. "Boy" was the lowest deckhand rank, so by this reckoning Edward J. Smith, the future Commodore of the White Star fleet, started his career on the lowest rung of the mercantile ladder and came up the hard way, "hands on" as the saying goes.

With a near relative as his first commanding officer, perhaps things were not so bad and it may be that Ted served a sort of unofficial apprenticeship under Captain Hancock and his mates. This would have put him in the best possible position for getting to "know the ropes" in his new job. This old nautical term that has fallen into common usage was basically what every sailor had to learn. The average sailing ship carried upwards of 200 different ropes and the purposes of each had to be committed to memory. Then there were the more technical branches of seamanship to be considered such as navigation, draught and displacement, the careful loading of ships and the science of keeping them balanced on an even keel. These, however, were not aspects of the job that could easily be fitted into the typical working day, so aspiring seamen, like most apprentices, had to study whenever they could and were probably forced to attend "crammer" sessions ashore, prior to sitting their exams. But above all, the young sailor needed to gain experience and get to know the moods and nuances of the sea and the differences that the open ocean and shallow or narrow waters presented.

Not only did life on a ship build the brain, but also it promoted brawn. Out in the open air, working at hard and physical jobs, day-in, day-out, seven days a week until the journey ended, unprepossessing boys could grow in a few years into muscular, barrel-chested men. Yet on the downside it might also be said that Ted Smith had adopted a very dangerous life. Besides the ever present menace of being washed overboard, the physical extremes of the job also took their toll — muscular strains were the most likely complaints, hernias were also common and there were illnesses and even death caused by exposure and dampness. It comes as little surprise, therefore, that the merchant navy was not seen as a prudent choice so far as career prospects were concerned.

But, if the sailor was spared injury or illness and had the wits to get on, there was a wealth of experience to be gained from such a life and there was the advantage that you got to see the world as few others did. Certainly the romance of travel must have gained many recruits for the sea.

Ted spent over three and a half years aboard the Senator Weber, first as boy, but from 9th February 1868 onwards, probably due to the influence of his half-brother, he served as the ship's (uncertified) 3rd mate. This position may have gained him the luxury of his own cabin in the aft of the ship, a room of his own in which to concentrate on his studies.

Ted stayed with the Senator Weber until 3rd September 1870. He then took a break of over a month, probably taking another trip home before returning to sea as an able seaman. The usual route of promotion for a sailor was from boy to ordinary seaman before the sailor could aspire to the working rank of able seaman. However, it was as a fully-fledged able seaman that Ted signed on aboard the Halifax, Nova Scotia-registered vessel, the Amoy, on 18th October.

The life of an able seaman was far different from the cushioned and comparative luxury of a mate's cabin. When he got aboard ship, Ted found his quarters in the cramped forecastle. The fo'c'sle, as it was generally called, was formed and confined by the pointed bow of the vessel; it was generally spartan in aspect, unheated and with little in the way of ventilation. Men slept upwards of eight to a cabin on bare wooden bunks; their only belongings were the clothes they wore (and usually slept in – changing was made very difficult in such cramped quarters) and a few personal items they may have carried in a sea chest, which could be lashed to the floor by iron rings. The sailor brought his own mattress (usually stuffed with straw), oilskins (rough weather garments – usually gaiters, a jacket and a hat) and a few oddments such as a knife, fork, spoon, soap and a brush.

The fo'c'sle was the centre of society on a ship, but it was unhygienic except when it was washed out by the sea which during rough weather usually found its way into this inner sanctum. All too often the shared quarters were filled with the heavy smells of dirt and worse if illness took a hold. Baths were rare except when the ship was becalmed in tropical waters when the men could take a dip in the sea itself; personal hygiene was more often than not confined to each man taking a cold scrub out of a ship's bucket. Nor was the food aboard such voyages anything to write home about, consisting per man, per day of a ration of about a pound and a half of dry salted beef, or pork that had often been stored for years, and a supply of hardtack – tough, rock-like ship's biscuits that more often than not were infested with weevils. The ship's cook sometimes provided more appetising meals, such as a duff pudding of bread and fat steamed in a linen bag. There might be a few extra luxuries – occasionally apples were carried in barrels and unleavened bread could be cooked up at a pinch. On top of all of this, every twelve days, a ration of lime juice was served out to every man to prevent scurvy.

The able seamen were formed into watches; the mate was in charge of the port watch that looked after the port side and the bowsprit and trimmed the sails on the foremast, while the starboard watch under the 2nd mate tended the starboard ropes and the rear of the ship including the main and mizzenmasts. All of the sailors turned out to set sail and then worked alternate watches, with one watch looking to the sails and steering, while the off-watch ate or slept. Providing the weather remained good, this system operated without interruption for the rest of the journey. The duties whilst on watch could include a stint at the wheel, but the time was usually spent tending the canvas, making sure that the ropes were taut and untangled and that they were not sawing each other to bits. Scrubbing the decks and greasing the anchor chains were also duties regularly carried out. Generally, such jobs were not designed to improve the speed of the ship, but to make sure that the ship was "ship-shape", in other words, ready for anything.

The majority of a seaman's duty was, however, the setting and furling of the sails. Setting sail was easy; the canvas was merely let loose from the yards and after it was dropped, the sail was trimmed to the wind under the supervision of the mate or master. The position of the sail was then fixed by using the running rigging, the lengths of rope used to secure the sails to the sides of the ship. These ropes were apart from the standing rigging and the ladder-like shrouds that were attached to each mast. When the sails needed to be furled, though, especially in rough weather, the riggers were ordered aloft. They climbed up the shrouds with their backs to the wind so that they were pressed against the rigging, until they reached the yardarm. Quickly, the men transferred their weight from the shroud to the footline beneath the spar and gripping onto the yard, they legged their way along. When everyone was ready, the canvas was slackened off and the corners were winched up to the yard, leaving the sagging belly of the sail to be taken in by hand. Letting go with his hands and supported only by the footline and his stomach resting on the spar, each sailor reached down and grabbed a handful of canvas and hauled it up under his stomach until each man was resting on a cushion of canvas, Moreover, the sails were not made of a thin, light material, but of a heavy duty weave, sometimes double-thickness, not far removed in texture from tarpaulin, so the rigours that such a duty entailed, especially if the canvas was wet or if the job had to be done in a storm, could be crippling. Then, when the entire mass of sail was drawn up, it was rolled, beaten and finally lashed down.

It could be a terrifying experience, especially for those inexperienced in such a job, but the time-served sailor knew his duty and took a sort of pride in the speed and ability of his furling. He also knew that despite being suspended several storeys above the rolling deck or hanging over an angry sea, being aloft for all the perils it engendered did have advantages over being down on the storm-lashed deck, where towering waves could engulf the ship and pick a man off the deck for him never to be seen again. Such was the life of a sailor.

Ted Smith spent nearly five months aboard the Amoy, until 6th March 1871, and then served close on four months, again as an able seaman, aboard the Liverpool-registered vessel, Madge

Wildfire, after joining her on 24th March. In these vessels, Ted went wherever the cargo needed to go. For instance, the Amoy was registered in Nova Scotia, so perhaps she took on the north Atlantic; certainly the ships of Andrew Gibson & Co. operated between Britain, Europe and South America.

When Ted left the Madge Wildfire on 15th July 1871, he had clocked up 4 years, 11 months and 26 days at sea; his seagoing initiation was over and he seems to have felt that it was time to move onwards and upwards. During this early part of his time at sea, his home life was unsettled and he was lodged at the Sailors' Home in Liverpool when he could not get back to Hanley. What kind of life he led is unknown. The traditional sailor's portside pastimes lasted as long as his money did, most of which was spent on drinking and wenching, but as to whether these were the sort of sports Ted went in for is open to debate. When he could get away from Liverpool, though, he did and often returned to Hanley, usually accompanied by his half-brother. The Smiths' grocer's store had moved to 30 Well Street, an address that no longer exists, but it was there that Ted and Joseph Hancock, both listed as seamen, were resident when the census was taken in 1871. However, there was no time for wine, women or relatives when Ted left the Madge Wildfire; instead he returned to his bunk at the Sailors' Home and prepared as best he could for the exam for a 2nd mate's certificate of competency.

The ambitious young sailor applied for his examination on 21st July 1871; the next day he paid an exam fee of £1 and two days after that sat the exam. It consisted of three parts: navigation, seamanship and commercial code signals. Sections such as these tested the applicant's knowledge not only of practical seamanship but also the "rules of the road" of sea travel. Ted took his exam on 24th July, passed all three sections (failure in any one of the three meant that the entire exam was failed) and received his certificate on 12th August that year. With his certificate came his registration number, 14102. Twelve days later, he signed on board the Liverpool-registered vessel, Record, serving as her 2nd mate.

As a 2nd mate, Ted had charge of the starboard watch, but his duties included much more than that and it was his job to supervise the work of the men during the day as well as during his own watch; he was essentially a type of qualified foreman. As a mate he was again out of the cramped fo'c'sle and back aft in the comparative comfort of his own cabin. Ted left the Record on 19th January 1872, but in his capacity as a 2nd mate, he also served aboard two other vessels: the Agra, registered in the Windward Isles, from 28th February to 27th July 1872, and the Quebec-registered N. Mosher, from 27th September 1872 to 3rd March 1873.

He then decided to put in for the exams that would gain him his 1st mate's certificate of competency. Before a sailor could even apply to be tested, he had to clock up the necessary time as an officer in charge of a watch, so evidently, Ted had gained enough experience in the two-year period he had served as a 2nd mate. During that time Ted had left home for good and when he paid the 10s. exam fee on 22nd March 1873, he was living at 5 Hanover Street, Liverpool. The exams were the same as before but at a more advanced level and he sat them three days later and again passed them all. He received the certificate of competency on 8th April whilst in Bremerhaven in Germany, though why and how he had gone there is unknown.

The duties of the 1st mate were many. The job of the captain was the safe sailing and positioning of the ship, but it was up to the mate to see that the skipper's orders were carried out swiftly and to the best advantage. The mate was essentially in charge of the day-to-day running and maintenance of the vessel, measuring her speed, and in charge of the soundings when the ship came into coastal waters. As an experienced navigator, he carried out many of the duties of the captain, whose job, should anything have happened to him, the mate was expected to take over. But above all he was the mouth of the captain, so when the weather turned sour and the captain decided that the situation warranted it, it was to the mate that he gave the order to call 'All hands', and it was the mate who supervised the setting and the furling of the sails. These, amongst many others, were the duties Ted carried out between 1873 and 1875 during three terms aboard the square-rigged, Liverpool-registered sailing ship, the Arzilla, which he joined on 15th July 1873.

When he had finished his third term aboard the Arzilla on 4th May 1875, Ted applied for the exams for the master's ordinary certificate of competency. On 19th May 1875, he handed over his £2 exam fee and three days later sat and again passed all three sections of the exams. On 26th May 1875, he picked up his certificate in Liverpool and became a fully-fledged master mariner.

Now a point of contention arises. Having gained his master's certificate, was he given a command straight away, or was he, as the evidence suggests, forced to wait a year before commanding his first ship? Many later reports had him as commanding his first vessel at the age of 25 (he was 25 when he received his certificate). Yet, when in 1888, he applied for his extra master mariner's certificate, Smith claimed that it was in May 1876 – a full year after receiving his certificate – that he first got his own ship. She was one of Andrew Gibson's South American traders, the Lizzie Fennell.

The Lizzie Fennell is described in various accounts as a 'ship' and 'full-rigged'; Smith himself described the 1,040-ton trader as a 'ship', which gives us a good idea of what his first command was like. The word "ship" has become descriptive of all kinds of large ocean-going vessels, but when used in its strictest nautical terms it describes a certain type of vessel. In the days of sail, ships were not determined by their hull, but by their rig, which was usually the part of the ship best seen over the horizon by other vessels. The smallest craft was the schooner, which never carried square sails and was an American development. Next up was the brigantine with a square rig on the foremast and rigged in fore-and-aft fashion (i.e. with triangular or trapezoid sails) on the mainmast. As the amount of square rig and masts increased on a ship so did the description. Bigger than a brigantine was the brig, then came the barquentine with three masts, then the barque and finally the ship. The ship was qualified by being full-rigged, in other words the masts fore, main and mizzen carried the classic square (or rather rectangular) sails which were stretched on yardarms and it also carried triangular sails and a large boom sail on the mizzenmast. A later development on the full-rigged ship was the clipper ship, which had cleaner lines and a knife-like bow that "clipped" through the water. So, from just these two descriptions of the Lizzie Fennell it's fair to presume that Ted Smith, at the age of 26, had at his command a very large, full-rigged, three-masted, high seas trading ship.

Of Smith's life aboard the Lizzie Fennell, only a little is known. We know that his 1st mate on at least some of his voyages was a man named Sinclair, a sailor of some ability, who later served on board under Captain Hancock and who in time himself became the skipper of the Lizzie Fennell. It was Sinclair who was in command of the ship when she caught fire and had to be abandoned in mid-Atlantic. Another man under Smith's command, at least during his final years with the ship, was his nephew, James William Sidney Harrington, the son of William and Thirza. In later life, "J.W.S.", as he was known by reporters, did not mention anything untoward having happened to the Lizzie Fennell whilst it was under his uncle's command, though he vividly remembered having served under Sinclair during the ship's final voyage.

As captain over his crew, Smith was master of all he surveyed – it was no idle boast that a ship's captain was next in line to God where the good of his ship was concerned. However, the rank of ship's captain did have its disadvantages: it was a very lonely position, the holder being exiled so often from his family and friends whilst at sea and from his crew by his rank. Ultimately, it was the captain who took overall responsibility if a ship was badly sailed or damaged, or if the navigation had been faulty and these were the charges laid at Smith's feet when the Titanic sank. Yet it was also the job of the captain to be bold, to force a passage, run storms and navigate reefs and find the trades that carried the ships on.

To counter this, there were comforts: the captain, as with his mates, had his own cabin, which was by far the most luxurious aboard. This cabin and the mates' were situated around a communal saloon under a skylight where the master and his lieutenants enjoyed the comforts of eating at a table and sitting upon upholstered benches.

A full complement for a ship was about 35 to 40 men and boys, most of them being "riggers", able seamen such as Smith himself had been, who worked the watches and who could be called on day or night. There were a few men on each ship, though, who only worked during the day and had the night off unless 'All hands' was called. The ordinary seamen knew them as "idlers", but the jobs they carried out were essential for the smooth running of the ship. The ship's carpenter, or "chippie", was needed on all wooden ships, while "sails" was the sailmaker, a man of considerable skill who tended and patched the miles of canvas that each ship carried. Most important of all was the cook, irreverently known as the "doctor" – after all, ships, like armies, marched, or rather sailed, on the stomachs of the men that sailed them.

It took a special kind of man to command a ship and a man of exceptional ability and leadership to gain his own vessel at the age of 26, with virtual lordship over a crew of big, brawny old "salts", who looked as hard as they worked and swore. The ladder of promotion in the merchant navy was notoriously slow and tortuous. The step from apprentice or seaman to 2nd mate could be easily achieved, as there were plenty of berths for junior officers, and most aspiring sailors could hold a master's certificate by their late 20's. However, it was a fortunate man indeed who secured a berth as 1st mate before his mid-30's and to become a ship's captain below 40 was virtually unheard of. So, when Smith took command of the Lizzie Fennell, it was not surprising to find some of the older men chaffing at him for being so young and in command of a ship. However, Smith replied with some wit that youth was something he would soon grow out of. From boy to ship's captain, he had indeed come up the hard way, but his obvious intelligence and hard work had allowed him to master every problem that his chosen career had thrown his way; he had learnt the ropes and grown accustomed to life at sea, he understood navigation and code signals and had gained the ability to lead – all of this marked him out as something more than an ordinary sailor.

Smith commanded the Lizzie Fennell (often wrongly referred to as the "Lucy Fennell") for almost four years and seems in that time to have proved the point that age was no barrier to skill. His ship appears to have led a blameless existence sailing the South American trades, shipping goods to and from British Colonies and ports such as Montevideo and Buenos Aires. Without a doubt the

Lizzie Fennell was a cargo ship, as the coveted passenger service had even by that time passed firmly over to the new steamships. It seems likely that Smith even got to take his ship around Cape Horn. The Horn was not yet solely the province of the hardy windjammer, nor was it favoured by steamer travel.

Cape Horn had a bad reputation among sailors and was unanimously disliked because of its high winds (channelled between Antarctica and South America), ferocious seas, treacherous shoals and merciless breakers. When ships coasting along in the Roaring Forties latitudes came into sight of the iron-grey cliffs of the Horn, where the Andes tumble into the sea, they knew that they were in for a bad time. Hatches and portholes were battened down, loose deck fittings were secured and the ships' sails were stripped off to be replaced with a second best set. The men put on their oilskins and the ship pulled on full rig to try and make the passage of the Horn as short, swift and sweet as possible. Even on a good day the sea was choppy, but at its worst, as in the words of an old song, the unforgiving Horn would make sailors 'wish they'de never been born'. Storms were usual, accompanied by anything from driving rain, to heaving seas, snow, sleet and hail like grape-shot, and even rogue icebergs could be encountered. Even wrapped in waterproofs, with the decks constantly awash, men were soaked to the skin, but they could not leave their work and strained at the ropes, fighting their ship through the tempest, trimming each sail to catch the erratic winds. Not surprisingly, the Horn was a ship's graveyard, but if Smith ever commanded his ship on such a passage, he proved himself equal to the demands required.

The captain's greatest responsibility was always the safety of his ship and crew, but next came the speed and efficiency of the service his ship provided. For a quick journey, a master needed above all to be an astute navigator. In our computer age, where satellites miles above the earth can pinpoint even small objects on the ground, it is perhaps hard to imagine how men piloted their ships so accurately across featureless oceans, aided only by a few nautical instruments and a series of small-scale maps even on the longest voyage.

Every captain needed several instruments, which he was

expected to provide for himself: a sextant, a ship's chronometer (a very expensive form of clock, which was usually designed to be watertight; it was carried in its own box and was set to Greenwich Mean Time at the start of each voyage) and a telescope, or later a pair of binoculars, to watch out for dangers and other ships.

At noon each day, in order to check the ship's position at sea, Smith had to get out his sextant to "shoot the sun". The angle of the sun – if it could be seen – compared with the earth allowed the captain to calculate his latitude with a reasonable degree of accuracy. Longitude was calculated by referring to the chronometer and comparing its GMT time to the day and night times they were experiencing at sea. However, sextants, and especially clockwork chronometers, were like all instruments of that nature, prone to interference from wear, humidity, dampness and motion, so the captain often had to play things by ear.

Measuring the ship's speed was another way of calculating, at least approximately, a ship's place in the world. For this, the skipper would order the ship's log to be heaved astern. The log (originally a wooden spar or log, but later a canvas cone) was thrown overboard on the end of a rope. This rope was wound up on a spindle, which was held aloft by a crewman, and knotted at regulated intervals along its length. The 1st mate stood by the ship's rail, letting the slack slip through his hand, but when his hand reached a marker rag on the rope, at his command another crewman turned over a sandglass which measured out a set number of seconds during which the mate let the rope slip unhindered through his hand. The length of time was usually 14 to 28 seconds and in that time the mate counted the number of knots that passed on the rope. By tallying these knots, the ship's speed in nautical miles could be measured (a nautical mile, or knot, is approximately 800 feet longer than a mile on land). By such "dead-reckoning" every 24 hours, an eye on the ship's compass and the measurements by sextant and chronometer, the good captain could get his bearings in the middle of the largest of oceans, so though often inaccurate, such a system of navigation obviously worked and even today still forms a large part of the training for would-be navigators.

SAIL AND STEAM

This routine carried on for almost four years and Smith seems to have enjoyed his job. Certainly he appears to have recalled his few years with the Lizzie Fennell with some fondness in later times, no doubt because she was his first command, and sailing in sunnier climes with the wind at his back and spending time in the decadent and exotic ports of call surely seemed a life away from the later north Atlantic service of his career. But there was ambition, always that burning ambition onwards and upwards, and as he was blessed with the capacity to succeed, Smith seems to have seen no need to stop where he was. He had grown aware of the advantages of making a career for himself with the big shipping companies whose luxury steamers operated out of Liverpool. For the ambitious sailor there were two great companies to choose from: the Cunard Line, which held the edge in speed, and the White Star Line, which operated the most luxurious of all steamers. It was the White Star Line whose ships had caught Smith's imagination; their black and white ships with the distinctive black and yellow funnels were regular visitors to Liverpool's docks and it was the sight of one of their classiest vessels that finally took him away from the sailing ships of Andrew Gibson & Co.

In January 1880, the Lizzie Fennell returned from her latest voyage, perhaps another jaunt to South America. At the approach to Liverpool a cutter came alongside and Smith welcomed aboard the Liverpool harbour pilot. Many port authorities, especially those with difficult approaches or complex harbours, often required the presence of a pilot aboard vessels in their waters, to advise the captain as he guided his ship into dock. On this occasion, Smith stood chatting with the pilot, noting as he did so some of the other vessels they passed. Around them stood a forest of masts and lines, but here and there the more compact shape of a passenger steamer. One of these they sailed past was the White Star steamship S.S. Britannic which was moored up to the company pier. The Britannic was a beauty by the standards of the time; she weighed 5,004 tons, was 455 feet long and her graceful outline was dominated by two large funnels amidships. The ship was six years old, held records of $7\frac{1}{2}$ days for both the passages west and eastbound to the United States and since her launch, had with her sister ship, the Germanic, served as the flagship of the White Star Line's transatlantic run. The luxury of her appointments and the prestige she promoted for her crew were the talking points of the shipping world and left passengers mightily impressed. Now the glamour of this ship fixed itself on Smith. He pointed her out to the pilot and said words to the effect that he 'would not mind going down a rung or two', if he could serve aboard and eventually get to command such a fine vessel. Such was the effect on Smith that he was later reported as having resigned as the captain of the Lizzie Fennell almost as soon as the ship had moored. Several days later, he managed to get a tour of the glamorous Britannic which finally made up his mind for him. Two months later, in March 1880, Smith joined the White Star Line.

White Star no longer exists. In the 1930s the company merged with its arch-rival, Cunard, and was later totally submerged within that company. But in its heyday the White Star Line was one of the most prestigious shipping companies in the world, giving an assurance of steady travel and luxury accommodation. The company had humble beginnings. In 1845, 25-year old John Pilkington had begun business on his own account and soon entered into partnership with fellow entrepreneur, Henry Threlfall Wilson. The two men set up a shipping concern given over to transporting emigrants and cargo between Liverpool and Australia. This began in 1852 and the company expanded in business (and riches) when its ships were used to transport gold from this far-flung colony. The partnership changed in 1857, when James Chambers replaced Pilkington, but the trade done by the original fleet of clippers continued unabated. In 1864, the partnership of Wilson and Chambers (the White Star Line) invested in its first steamship, the Royal Standard, while the company itself was undergoing transformation, eventually ending up (just as the Royal Standard was on its maiden return from Australia) as the Liverpool, Melbourne and Oriental Steam Navigation Co. Ltd.

However, so many changes in the company structure weakened confidence in its service and the line began to find itself seriously in debt. A further change came in 1865 when John Cunningham replaced Chambers, while in 1866 a bank failure crippled the White Star company. Like so many other small companies that had got off to a good start, things got shaky when its circumstances changed. The collapse, when it came, was total. In 1868 the company assets were sold, the trembling Wilson and Cunningham partnership was dissolved and the White Star Line would have just been a memory had not the company name and symbol – a red, swallow-tailed pennant bearing a five-pointed white star – been bought up by a young Liverpool shipowner named Thomas Henry Ismay.

Ismay was what can only be described as a dedicated business-man and only a year after the purchase of the White Star goodwill and flag, his partner, George H. Fletcher, completed negotiations with the Harland and Wolff firm of shipbuilders in Belfast to build the fleet's first four steamships. On 6th September 1869, the company (the official name of which was the Oceanic Steam Navigation Company Ltd.) was registered with over £400,000 in capital.

The new ships (the first being the Oceanic) were given over not to the old Australian run, but were placed on the north Atlantic service to America, a run that was already popular with a number of other emergent shipping companies. The company started slowly, but gradually began to build up a clientele. Then, disaster struck. On 1st April 1873, the second of these new ships, the Atlantic, struck the breakers off the island of Marr's Head off Nova Scotia. Delayed by storms, Captain Williams had found the ship's coal supply almost exhausted and had tried to make it to Halifax, but the ship had been grounded and rapidly began to list to starboard. There were screams for the men to make for the rigging as water flooded the stern, drowning everyone unlucky enough to be in there. The storm still raged and it all took place at night. Some crewmen managed somehow to get ashore and with the brave assistance of local fishermen and their families, boats and lines were sent out to the survivors who still clung to the rigging and the few bare rocks that jutted out above the sea. The rescue attempts carried on throughout the night, but just before dawn the ship broke right behind the foremast. Over 400 people survived, but approximately 565 people perished; there were no women survivors and only one child. Prior to events that were to overtake the Titanic, it was the worst peacetime disaster at sea.

However, the company survived this catastrophe and still remembered the victims of the Atlantic in 1915, after the Titanic had sunk, when the company founded a memorial to them. But business carried on and when the new breed of steamers, such as the Britannic and the Germanic, came onto the scene, the fortunes of the White Star Line were again on the upturn and their ships gained their reputation for splendour.

Smith's master's certificate had served him well and enabled him to rise quickly to the command of a ship in the smaller sailing vessels of Andrew Gibson & Co. The White Star Line, though, operated a high-class liner and steamer service; their large ships needed considerable skill from a commander and the charge of such vessels was usually the province of qualified extra master mariners. Not only did an officer need skill as a seaman, but catering to the rich and famous, as well as being available to help the second and third-class passengers, required a certain polish in an officer that was perhaps first felt to be lacking in Smith. Therefore, for the first few years with his new employers, he found himself serving what amounted to a second apprenticeship as a junior officer on several White Star vessels.

Smith's career was destined to remain in the service of the north Atlantic run and only on a few occasions in the future did he ever get away from the western ocean mail boats and passenger liners. Not that being an officer on the north Atlantic run was a bad thing – indeed, most officers dreamed of such a chance, for the luxury steamers that plied the profitable route from Liverpool to New York were considered to be not only the finest ships in the company, but the finest in the entire merchant navy. Yet Smith did not straightaway get his first wish, to serve aboard the glamorous Britannic, but instead was employed as fourth and later third officer aboard the S.S. Celtic, a comfortable, but far less noticeable ship than the former. The Celtic had been launched in 1872, weighed 3,867 tons and measured 437 feet in length. She could carry up to 900 passengers in reasonable style and cruising along at full speed, she could make about 14 knots.

No major mishaps accompanied Smith's time aboard his first White Star liner, though of course there were storms, but having sailed the seas in far flimsier craft than the iron-hulled Celtic, it is doubtful whether these worried him. Still, the storms whipped up by the Atlantic could be spectacular, especially in winter. Charles Herbert Lightoller, a future officer of the White Star Line, described service aboard a western ocean mail boat in winter time as 'a kill or cure'. Ships in the early days were smaller, so were proportionally far more rigid in comparison with their larger descendants. This inherent toughness, a seeming invulnerability to anything that the weather could throw at the ships, meant that every captain felt that every effort could be made to force a passage, no matter what faced him. Smith on board the Celtic would have found out this truth during those early voyages, but especially on that which took place between 1st and 6th December 1881, when the ship ran a gauntlet of continuous mid-Atlantic hurricanes during her crossing from Liverpool to New York. For six days the Celtic struggled on gamely through mountainous seas, driving winds and terrible rolling waves that left the decks constantly awash and smashed some of her boats.

In such weather, nothing was safe – the wind could flatten steel crow's-nests against the mast as if they were made of paper, while seas could rip hatch covers off the deck and hurl them high into the air, or wreck the deck machinery. As a precaution, at least over the officers' quarters which were by far the most exposed, thick nets were spread to break up the waves as they came down, while the portholes had little oak shutters to protect them. These bull's-eye portholes were particularly vulnerable when a vessel shipped a sea.

Lightoller, such a valuable source of stories describing the life led by the average White Star officer at sea, told a story of one of his ships crashing through a wave whipped up by a typical winter storm that smashed the protective netting, bashed in the oak shutters and blew out the glass porthole, a piece of which shot across the room like a bullet and took the cup out of the hand of an officer who was sitting drinking tea by his table. Mealtimes in a rolling sea were even worse, being similar to doing gymnastics, and Lightoller recalled a further amusing story about a roast of beef that was catapulted off its trolley when the ship gave a violent heave, before it gracefully arced ten feet into the air and came to rest on a fellow officer's bunk. This incident was caused by the ship's propeller leaving the sea, which according to Lightoller, felt like dropping down the lift shaft in an express elevator. It was sensations of this sort that the passengers and crew of the Celtic must have experienced. Eventually, though, with its cargo of "killed or cured" passengers, the Celtic arrived in New York. All 302 of them disembarked, no doubt overjoyed to have reached terra firma.

During these early voyages, Smith also had ample time to grow used to the power structure in use aboard steamships and liners, which was far more diverse than the hierarchy found on cargo vessels. Of course the captain was still next to God, but beneath him, power was farmed out more evenly amongst a number of executive officers and heads of departments. As the fourth and later third officer on board the Celtic, Smith was one of the odd-bodies officially designated as navigation trainees, but it is best to start at the top and work our way down.

Under the master of every steamship served a number of bridge officers, principally his navigation staff. In number these could be anything up to eight (on the Titanic there were seven officers under the master). The chief officer was essentially another master, whose duty it was to act in the captain's place in any capacity, though he also had specific tasks, such as ensuring that his vessel was always in a state of equilibrium, a duty that a conscientious officer like Chief Officer Wilde saw fit to carry out even as the Titanic was sinking. The chief officer was usually, like the captain, an extra master mariner. Next came the first officer, whose job was that of an assistant to the chief, while the second officer was usually in charge of navigating the ship (though due to a shake-up in the power structure, the latter was not the case for Lightoller when he was the second officer of the Titanic). On modern vessels there is usually a first, a second and a third officer, the third officer normally being a trainee navigator, while undoubtedly aboard the big White Star ships, the third to sixth officers were navigation trainees. These men also acted as aides-de-camp to the captain.

On an ocean liner the presence of an active number of deck officers served as useful reference points for the passengers, at the same time providing a good many young officers with the chance to hone their social graces.

Other departments on the ships had a similar organisation under their own chiefs. The chief steward was in charge of the stewards and stewardesses, who acted as personal room servants and chambermaids. The head chef organised the cooking facilities, while the head pantryman was in charge of the stores and both had several assistants. Perhaps the man with the greatest responsibility after the master and the chief officer, was the chief engineer. Like that of the master of the ship, the position of chief engineer was one earned through years of hard work and exemplary service. Under the chief engineer were several assistants, who increased in number with the size of the ship. These engineers, junior and senior, could number over 30 in the biggest ships, such as the Olympic and the Titanic. All of them were technically proficient marine engineers and they cared for the smooth running, servicing, fuelling and oiling of the engines. All of them were men who had not only served long careers at sea, but had also spent much time in machine shops and drawing rooms, looking over complex design specifications, and as with the progression of the navigation officers, each had had to sit exams to advance up the tortuous ladder of promotion.

Good work aboard the Celtic rewarded Smith with promotion and between March 1882 and March 1884, he served as the second officer aboard the 4,367-ton S.S. Coptic. The beginning of his service aboard the yearling Coptic coincided with the ship taking up the Pacific station, making the run from Liverpool to New Zealand and occasionally as far as South America. As second officer, Smith was the navigator for a trip that encompassed voyages through the Atlantic, the Mediterranean, the Suez Canal, the Red Sea, the Indian Ocean and finally the Pacific Ocean.

From March 1884 to July 1885, Smith – perhaps by then sporting the Victorian beard that would later distinguish him from the clean-shaven young officers of the early twentieth century – returned to the north Atlantic. It must have been one of his happiest times, as he had finally gained a berth aboard the ship he most admired, when he became the second officer aboard the S.S. Britannic.

In July 1885, though, he had to move on and he was appointed as the first officer aboard the S.S. Republic. The Republic was a modest-sized ship compared with the monsters Smith was later to command. She was one of that dying breed of vessels that seemed to present an unhappy amalgam of sail and steam; her single smokestack – a lonely concession to turbine power – seemed hidden amid the rigging of her four masts. 470 feet long and grossing 3,707 tons, she was nonetheless a neat four-cylinder single-screw passenger liner. She was also the ship destined to be Smith's first White Star command.

Smith had time to settle into his new duties before the Republic was chartered briefly to the Inman Line later that year. Smith appears to have stayed on the ship and it was during this period that he was involved in his first known maritime accident, albeit as a spectator. On 20th September 1885, the Republic was leaving New York harbour under the compulsory command of one of the harbour pilots. So too was the outward bound Cunard liner, the S.S. Aurania. As the two ships neared one another, what exactly happened is not clear, but certainly confusion arose in the minds of the harbour pilots, concerned as to what course the opposing ship was taking, and suddenly the two vessels collided. The Aurania's bow smashed into the side of the Republic's nose and left a large triangular gash, while the Cunard vessel received a heavy blow to the stern. Of the two, the Republic came off worst and had to be dry-docked for repairs before she could sail. The Aurania, though dented, was still intact and so sailed as normal.

On 29th December, Smith suffered a family tragedy with the death of his father, who had moved to Runcorn with Catherine, but about a year after this, a happier occasion took place during one of Smith's terms in port, when he invited his old school friend Spencer Till to meet him in Liverpool. Upon their meeting, Smith treated Till to a personal tour of the Republic, before introducing him to a young woman in his company, announcing to his friend that they were engaged to be married. The three of them then went to see an exhibition being held in Liverpool.

At St. Oswald's Church, a tall, spired Normanesque edifice in the village of Winwick (pronounced "Winnick"), on Thursday 13th January 1887, Edward John Smith married Sarah Eleanor Pennington. She was the daughter of the late William Pennington, a local farmer, was a native of Winwick and bore a surname that was well represented among the local farmers. Eleanor, as she preferred to be called, was 26 years old, ten years Smith's junior, and a slim, strikingly handsome woman, brown-haired and fresh-faced, with a thin pointed nose. She had one of those faces that aged very gracefully. In a photograph of her taken in about 1903 (in Gibbs' "The Deathless Story of the Titanic"), she is seated with her infant daughter Helen on her lap. Eleanor, though about 42 in 1903, could have easily passed as a woman in her early thirties. In the picture she does have a rather starched formality as do most figures in Victorian or Edwardian photos, but those many years earlier at her wedding she would have cut a far different figure.

The couple were married after banns by the curate, James Carson. On the marriage certificate Smith signed himself as resident at Tuebrook and among his other details put down that his late father had been a potter, rather than a grocer as might have been expected. The only other matter of note is that they called a large number of witnesses for their marriage – five rather than the required two. These were: Thomas Jones, a brewer from Runcorn; Smith's half-brother, Joseph Hancock; John William Pennington; Maria Annie Pennington and one Mary Privett Rooker.

Immediately after the wedding the couple set up home locally in a square-fronted cottage that still exists today. There they mixed the honeymoon lovemaking with the more practical homemaking. However, for some reason, perhaps because it would give Smith a little more time at home with his new wife, they soon moved to Liverpool and within a couple of years were living at 39 Cambridge Road in Seaforth, a district that fronted the Liverpool docks.

On the intimate level, Eleanor called her husband 'Ted', or now and then more coyly, 'Teddy', while he affectionately and lovingly called her 'My only dear one'. After his years in a bachelor's existence Eleanor gave him a settled home life to return to. The two of them seem to have enjoyed a steady, happy marriage that survived and to some extent prospered, despite Smith's long periods at sea

In April 1887, almost as a wedding present, Smith was given temporary command of the S.S. Republic, but this did not last for long and in August he was transferred back to the glamorous Britannic as her popular first officer.

It was in February 1888 that Smith put himself forward to be tested for the extra master mariner's certificate of competency. On his first attempt on 14th February, for the first time in his career he failed an exam, losing out on the navigation section. Undaunted, he applied again three days later, well aware that the future success of his career depended on his passing these exams. On 20th February, he passed the tests and gained his certificate.

Also in 1888, Smith applied to and joined the ranks of the Royal Naval Reserve, the auxiliary force of merchant seamen, who in times of war, or during any other form of national emergency, could be called upon to serve as naval officers. After applying to join the R.N.R., prospective officers needed to undergo an official interview at the Admiralty in Whitehall. Smith was accepted. Normally, new officers were entered into the service as sub-lieutenants, but because he held a master's certificate Smith was qualified as a full lieutenant and it is in the full dress uniform of a lieutenant in the R.N.R. that he can be seen in the sepia-framed photograph which hangs in Hanley Town Hall. Once he had joined, Smith had the right to have the letters "R.N.R." after his name and providing a certain proportion of his crew were in the Reserve, his ship could thenceforth fly the blue ensign of the R.N.R., rather than the red ensign of the merchant navy. In future, if he was needed, Captain Smith could be trained and paid to serve in the Royal Navy. Shipping companies saw no harm in this practice as the individual's goodwill reflected on them. So, rather than being a liability, having men in the R.N.R. made good business sense.

3

Under The Blue Ensign

As an extra master mariner and with his rank in the R.N.R., Smith had earned the right to his own ship and he received his first permanent White Star command in April 1888. The ship he got was the S.S. Baltic, the 'little Baltic' as she eventually became known to distinguish her from her later, much larger namesake that Smith also went on to command.

Built in 1871, she was the twin sister to the Republic; White Star built most of its ships in pairs – the Baltic and Republic, the Germanic and Britannic etc., though occasionally there was a one-off such as the Oceanic, or a trio such as the Olympic, Titanic and the Gigantic, later renamed Britannic. The little Baltic grossed 3,707 tons and could touch over 15 knots flat out. She used on average 65 tons of coal a day, and, including a crew of 143, had accommodation for 1,309 people. She had been quite a ship in her heyday, having once gained the blue riband for her crossing of the Atlantic in 1873, in 7 days, 20 hours and 9 minutes. But by 1888, the Baltic was getting on and Smith was one of her last White Star captains, as later that year the ship was sold to the Holland American Line for £35,000. Renamed the Veendam, she continued in the Atlantic service for a further ten years, until she sank without loss of life after hitting a mid-Atlantic derelict in 1898.

After leaving the Baltic in May 1888, from June to September Smith briefly took command of the Britannic, but in December 1888, he took the new White Star cattle transporter Cufic out on her maiden voyage. In January 1889, he was back on the Republic as her full commander. There had been a few changes since he had last been on the ship – most notably a second-class section had been added. Second class drew a line between the opulence of first-class travel and the spartan accommodation offered by steerage. It was a sign of the times that it was mostly designed to cater for the professional classes and the wealthier working classes who increasingly took their business abroad, but who wanted cheaper travel than first class afforded though with more style and comfort than steerage. Again however, as with the Baltic, Smith seems to have been given command of the Republic merely to be one of those seeing her to the end of her White Star career. She too was sold to the Holland American Line for £35,000 and renamed the Maasdam, following the style of name change that her sister ship had undergone the year before. But before that came to pass, the Republic gave Smith the first test of the responsibility he had taken on as the commander of an ocean liner.

The incident happened on Smith's 39th birthday, 27th January 1889. The Republic arrived off Sandy Hook on the approach to New York Harbour and promptly ran aground. She was pretty firmly stuck and it took five hours of vigorous work on the part of the master and crew before the ship was finally refloated. After this delay, the Republic made speed to arrive at New York. When she finally moored up at the White Star pier and her passengers had all disembarked, the day seemed to have given Smith nothing more annoying than an upset journey, but suddenly tragedy struck. Down below in the boiler room, the furnace flue to a lower forward boiler fractured, perhaps due to the impact of the earlier grounding, and a spout of heat and flame shot into the room which was still crowded with firemen and stokers. Three men were killed instantly and seven others were badly injured. Ambulances were called for and the injured men were able to walk to them from the ship. The dead were removed and when the the fire was under control, it was drawn and damped down, then the steam let off from the boilers before an investigation could be made. It was a sad day all round, but life had to go on. An inspection was made of the damage done to the ship, but this was found to be minimal and the inspectors confidently predicted that it could be fully repaired and the ship ready for sea in a few hours.

Smith had now had his first few tastes of commanding ocean liners and over the next decade or so he found himself in charge of a succession of such vessels. From April 1889 to July 1889, Smith commanded the Celtic, then he took charge of the Coptic in the Australian service from December 1889 to December 1890. This command came to an end when he grounded the ship off Main Island, having departed from Rio de Janeiro en route to Plymouth, but this time there were no serious repercussions. Later in December 1890, Smith returned to the north Atlantic run as captain of the Adriatic. This command lasted until February 1891, then in March he briefly took the helm of the Runic for a month. May 1891 saw his return as captain of the Britannic. The Britannic still seems to have been the apple of Smith's eye and during one of his periods in charge of the ship, he sent a large framed photograph of her to Spencer Till, an act which seems to have shown his pride in having finally achieved this sought-after command. In June 1893, he left the ship for a month to captain the Adriatic, but by July, he was back with the Britannic. However, 1893 was a year punctuated with personal tragedy as Smith's mother, Catherine, died on 1st November, whilst Joseph Hancock, who had been working as the longshore superintendant for Andrew Gibson & Co., was killed by heart disease. Nevertheless, these events only briefly interrupted Smith's command of the Britannic.

In 1895, there was another short break from Smith's captaincy of the Britannic when for a period he was again in charge of the cattle transporter, Cufic, but on her arrival in Liverpool from New York on 17th January 1895, Smith reported the loss of 75 head of cattle during the voyage.

After this, Smith had a final stint in command of the Britannic, which ended in April 1895. May to June was spent in command of the S.S. Germanic, but in July 1895 he was appointed to command the 9,965-ton S.S. Majestic, whose bridge he found himself treading for most of the next nine years, making the Majestic his longest held command. Such an appointment was an accolade; Smith was good at his job and it must surely have been one he enjoyed – after all, the job of commanding a prestigious ocean liner was one of the most desired jobs in his profession.

The duties of a liner captain were completely different from the duties of a cargo captain on a sailing ship. Of course, the principal duty of the master was to his ship and crew, motivating the latter so that the former was operated smoothly. However, it was also the captain's duty to cultivate an image that would attract customers, especially among the rich and famous, many of whom would hopefully become regular, valued customers. So the captain was also a P.R. man for his shipping company. For the company, choosing a ship's captain was, therefore, not only a matter of picking the best qualified sailor, but also the best qualified host, diplomat, friend and confidant, sometimes marriage or finance counsellor, and friendly ear. However, the position of captain then, as now, gave power to many pompous and exacting martinets, men who cared more about getting the job done than treating their fellow workers like human beings.

Smith, though, found the perfect line; he was disciplined, but treated the members of his crew in a friendly manner. Sixth Officer Moody of the Titanic wrote to his sister about Captain Smith, saying, 'Though I believe he's an awful stickler for discipline, he's popular with everybody.' Also, a steward from the Titanic said of Smith, 'This crew knew him to be a good, kind-hearted man, and we looked upon him as a sort of father.' Perhaps the best recommendation, though, came from C.H. Lightoller. Lightoller had sailed with many captains and experienced the odd martinet or two, but he both liked and admired Smith, who lived up to his expectations in a sea captain, governing not by force, but by what Lightoller called 'accepted discipline, tact, his own personality and good common sense'. He described Smith, or "E.J." as he was generally known to his officers, as having a quiet and friendly nature and an invariably warm smile, which belied the image of the grizzled sea dog that his appearance seemed to convey. Not that Smith could not bark an order when he needed to, but usually it was not necessary, as both officers and crew liked him and he ran a happy ship. Lightoller, who lived until 1952, remembered Smith as the best sea captain he had ever known: 'He was a great favourite and a man any officer would give his ears to sail under.'

These recommendations show in a large way the secret of Captain Smith's success. A happy and efficient ship was, after all, far more pleasant to the passengers than a merely efficient ship. It was a style that marked Smith out at the very beginning of his career as a liner captain and gained him many admirers. Mr. and Mrs. John Thalton were an American couple impressed by the captain and their comments after his death reveal something of the bond that often grew up between a good ship's master and his passengers:

'We sailed with Captain Smith on the little Baltic of the White Star Line, the first transatlantic steamer which he ever commanded; and since then, a period of nearly thirty years, we have followed him from ship to ship ... We always felt so safe with him, for one knew how deeply he felt the responsibility of his ship and all on board. He has been a deeply cherished friend on sea and land all these years, and we hold him in love and veneration, and are proud that we could count so noble a man among our closest friends.'

Another seasoned traveller who grew friendly with Smith was the Right Reverend William Wilcox Perrin, the Bishop of Willesden, who crossed the Atlantic three or four times with him, and he felt Smith to have been, 'the truest and best friend of every seaman and fireman on his ship and [he] looked after steerage passengers as well as more favoured individuals.'

Steerage passengers were the third-class passengers that generally formed the bulk of those crossing the Atlantic; theirs were the cheapest berths on the ship, what on airliners are described as economy class. Most of the captain's time, though, was given over to catering for the first-class passengers. This was not really through favouritism, but economics. Though steerage passengers earned a shipping company its bread and butter, most steerage travellers would probably never cross the Atlantic again, as many were emigrants. However, the first-class, and later the second-class, passengers formed a regular core of income, their ranks being made up not only of nobility, but also of such people as salesmen, writers, journalists, lecturers and politicians, whose business demanded a great deal of travel, so the more comfortable a shipping company could make its journeys, the more they were likely to think well of the line and use it again. Pulling out all the stops in this respect meant that the ship's captain was identified as their host. The better the host and the service he gave, the more regular travellers the line gained and many, like the Thaltons, came to identify with their favourite captains, quite literally following them from ship to ship.

Therefore the captain's job was a cross between being a modern airline pilot and a hotel manager, who always had to be pleasant, presentable and confident. Of course, though, the journeys took longer than those of modern airline travel, so the captain received so much more exposure to the passengers, unless of course, the weather was sufficiently bad to keep the master constantly on the bridge. However, when the weather was good, the privilege of dining at the captain's table was sought after by the first-class passengers.

Some captains found these duties irksome and perhaps as a consequence, modern ocean liner captains have some help where the passengers are concerned, in that they have a staff captain who can help in accommodating the attentions of the passengers. However, invariably they still look up to the ship's master as their true host. Captains of modern cruise liners, such as those of Cunard's splendid Q.E.2, find themselves playing host to royalty, nobility and the stars of stage, screen and literature. Captain Smith in his time certainly entertained nobility, and possibly royalty, aboard his ships, where they were housed in suites that dripped luxury, where individual aspects of the rooms, even individual rooms themselves, were the products of renowned craftsmen. The beds, the panelling, the crockery, the fittings and the decor could all be separately made, but to suit an overall design.

Though Smith was too early to encounter any of the great Hollywood stars, he would certainly have had occasion to meet many of the great stars of the theatre and the music hall. Acting companies, for instance, carried on a brisk trade between Britain and America. Smith would have run across these during his terms as a junior officer, but more so as the captain. Perhaps the most famous of these acting companies in the nineteenth century was the Lyceum Theatre Company, whose leading players included two of the most respected actors of their generation, the mercurial Henry Irving and the beautiful, red-haired Ellen Terry. Between 1883 and 1907, the company took on eight tours of New York, where they received not only a constant warm welcome, but also rave reviews. The first of these tours, in 1883, began when the company boarded Smith's favourite ship, the Britannic, in Liverpool. (Ellen Terry in her autobiography "The Story of My Life" mistakenly called the Britannic a Cunard ship, but the only Cunard ship with a similar name, the Britannia, had been laid off in 1880.) With their retinue, as one of their managers, was a future celebrity, Bram Stoker, who in 1897 became something of an overnight sensation when his Gothic horror story "Dracula" was published. This tour, of course, was during the period when Smith was a junior officer, though he was not yet aboard the Britannic, but it is entirely possible that he greeted them as a ship's commander on their later tours.

All of this aside, it is still useful to take a look at a precis of Ellen Terry's adventures at sea, which reflect some of the experiences and preconceptions of the first-time traveller, as well as describing the scenes that occurred on each voyage, with the departure from Liverpool and the arrival in New York.

Many people had flocked to the docks to see them off on the tour, one of these being Oscar Wilde, who had just begun to curl his hair and who expressed the opinion that he had been 'disappointed in the Atlantic'. Then they were off, and Ellen launched into a delightful spree-like description of her first Atlantic voyage. She found sea travel enchanting and despite the ship rolling and rolling, through being loaded with pig-iron, she felt no ill effects, declaring herself 'a splendid sailor' and 'jolly at sea'.

Her ideas as to what she would meet in America are amusing, especially in her images concerning American women, whom she seems to have thought were kindred spirits to Calamity Jane, who wore red flannel shirts and carried bowie knives! She was also convinced that she was going to get mugged in the street. Her fears about New York being squalid and ugly were, however, pleasantly allayed. She was astounded by the spectacle and beauty of the harbour entrance, busy with steamers and ferries crowding up to the wharfs, while the Statue of Liberty rose up majestically amidst all this bustle. This, of course, was not the cityscape of modern-day New York, but there were a few landmarks that are still familiar to modern travellers, most notably the Brooklyn Bridge, which struck her as hanging over the harbour entrance like a vast spider's web.

When Smith took his ships into New York Harbour, it was with a style of his own, 'at full speed' according to Lightoller, recalling early service under him. This high-speed approach to New York was undertaken despite the slalom course that faced any vessel making the approach. A bank known as the South-West Spit was a particularly troublesome spot, but Lightoller said that when Smith brought his ship in the crew would 'fairly flush with pride'. Under Smith's hand the vessel was swung around, as the captain judged the distance between the sandbanks perfectly, with only a few feet to spare on either side. Lightoller approved of such a swashbuckling style of seamanship and it was one of the main reasons that he admired Smith as he did. The glorious high-speed entrance to New York Harbour gave the passengers an experience that they would remember, so it was no wonder they came back for more!

The captain of an ocean liner, like Smith, might encounter world-renowned singers and musicians, famous writers, sports stars and the big businessmen of Britain and America. White Star carried its fair quota of people who got to see as much of the world as Smith – famous adventurers and travellers in an age where there was still much to be discovered, politicians roving the world and journalists in search of the ever tempting story. For example, William T. Stead, journalist, spiritualist and seasoned traveller, often used White Star ships and probably counted as one of Smith's "regulars"; certainly the two of them were on friendly terms.

Stocky and bearded in appearance, Stead was one of those campaigning individuals thrown up by the Victorian era. Like Charles Dickens (who had also been a journalist), Stead campaigned against social issues which he thought were dangerous or reprehensible. Early in his career he had sought to expose the exploitation and virtual enslavement of young working-class children, who could be bought with relative ease from parents who were too poor to have scruples. Like Dickens, his campaigns were against the pervading Victorian mood of "telescopic philanthropy", and he pointed out that there were more immediate problems on the doorstep of society requiring far more drastic action than taking Christianity to Africa or a civil service to India.

Stead also campaigned against faulty laws and, as a regular ocean traveller, faults in maritime regulations and the trouble these could cause interested him a great deal. In 1886, as editor and contributor to the "Pall Mall" magazine, he wrote a tale of an ocean liner that sank and how and why lives were lost because of a shortage of lifeboats. The story ended with him commenting cryptically, 'This is exactly what might take place, and what will take place, if liners are sent to sea short of boats.' More telling still, especially in relation to Captain Smith, in 1892, he wrote another tale entitled "From the Old World to the New", which told the story of how a ship, the Ann and Jane, was wrecked and sank after hitting an iceberg. The few survivors sheltered on the iceberg until they were rescued by the White Star S.S. Majestic. According to Stead, Smith was then in command of the Majestic (which he may well have been) and Stead wrote in a description of his friend. More interesting still in retrospect, is the fact that Stead was later a passenger on another of Smith's ships, R.M.S. Titanic.

Weather and duties permitting, Smith may have spent plenty of time engaged in conversation with such people, whilst wandering the decks or eating at his selected table in the first-class restaurant, or meeting the passengers as they lounged in steamer chairs enjoying the sun. But, when the weather turned sour, as it often did in the north Atlantic, the passengers never saw the captain, as at such times his place was on the bridge. Ask men in the street what sailors of old most feared and the chances are that they would say storms, but storms, though dangerous, could be handled by a good ship and captain. For ships' captains, the oldest and most treacherous enemy was fog. Smith, like many other captains, had a great fear of fog or mist and during the voyage of the Titanic he was noted as having been concerned that it might make an appearance. Even today with satellite links and anti-collision radar, sea captains still express a fear of fog. An all-enveloping bank of mist suddenly cutting across a ship's course blinds it to small and large craft and breakers alike. The area around Newfoundland has always been particularly notorious for its terrible banks of fog, caused by the connection of the warm Gulf Stream and the cold Labrador Current. There the worst months are always April and May, when the more rapidly moving Gulf Stream meets the ice that the Labrador Current brings off the pole.

The biggest danger with fog, though, is collision with other ships and the White Star company had in its history many tales of its own ships suffering collision in fog. In September 1880, the Baltic sailed out of a fogbank and ran into a schooner. In May 1887, another two of Smith's old ships, the Celtic and Britannic, met in a dense fog, with the former ramming the latter, which began to take in water. Four of the Britannic's passengers were killed and the rest had to be hastily transferred to the less seriously damaged Celtic. In 1907, the White Star ship, Romanic, ran over a fishing schooner, killing three of her eighteen crew. Four more people died when the Georgic collided with the American liner, Finance, off Sandy Hook, New Jersey in 1908. Even towards the twilight years of the White Star Line's existence, fog was still a great hazard for even the most reliable and visible ships, as shown in 1934, when the Olympic, the Titanic's elder sister, rammed and sank the Nantucket lightship. The Olympic was cruising at only ten knots and sounding her siren, as was the small, stationary, bright red ship with "NANTUCKET" written in white along her side. Yet even these precautions were not enough and in the collision, seven of the lightship's crew of eleven were killed.

In "Hard Times", written in 1854, Charles Dickens had written, 'It is the drifting icebergs setting with any current anywhere, that wreck the ships.' In a story that had nothing to do with the sea, Dickens had used a piece of well-known nautical folklore, namely that ships and ice and icebergs do not mix. Old sea songs and sailors' shanties were rife with tales of ships that had braved ice fields but had met their doom. Yet despite the fact that it was a well-known danger, ice came well down on a captain's list of worries, at least as long as his ship met ice alone, unaccompanied by storms or fog. It was not that White Star had not had trouble with icebergs. The company's first steamship, the Royal Standard, a full-rigged, three-masted, iron-hulled ship which carried a back-up steam-engine, had been sailing the south Pacific Ocean, when on 4th April 1864, she received a severe mauling from a truly monstrous berg that rose 'upwards of 600 feet' out of the water. The ship took on the berg with her starboard bow before being dragged like a rag doll along the side of the passing mountain of ice. Two masts snapped and things looked bad, but the berg cast the ship off. Amazingly, despite having been so viciously assaulted, the Royal Standard did not make water, which certainly says something for mid-Victorian shipbuilding.

When White Star came to run the prestigious route to New York, they found that bergs were also a problem there. Huge fields of ice were a regular obstruction to shipping from March through to May, with April being undoubtedly the worst month. But the bergs that formed the hard core of these ice fields were not considered so immediate a danger as fog or storm and in calm clear weather they did not appear to demand the total attention of the master. Icebergs were big, visible and seemingly easy to avoid, especially with the antidote of the steam-engine, which could take a ship across or against the current that dictated the berg's movements. They were still best avoided, though, and most skippers felt that this could be done with just the standard lookout and without needing to reduce speed.

As icebergs have so much of a part to play in this story, it is perhaps best to know something about them. They are fragments of Arctic or Antarctic glaciers and most of those in the north Atlantic are "calved" from the ragged outer edges of Greenland glaciers. The bergs, like the glaciers from which they come, are many thousands of years old, formed from layer upon layer of super-compacted ice, which originally fell as snow far inland and was gradually pushed seawards as the ice sheet increased. In the manner in which it was laid down, glacial ice resembles sedimentary rock in composition and it is not surprising to find that it also has round about the same density as solid rock and is easily capable of ripping and puncturing sheet steel as if it were cardboard.

The bergs that form when they break from the ice sheet vary in size; some can measure upwards of a thousand feet out of the water, despite seven-eighths of an iceberg being beneath the surface, while the smallest classification of an iceberg, known to sailors as a "growler", can be a mere 15 feet out of the water. These growlers are usually broken fragments of larger bergs and are by far the most numerous in any ice field. Along with the bergs there are smaller chunks of ice known as floe ice, as well as a crystalline covering of frozen sea water.

By its nature ice is a gregarious substance and where there is one type of ice, others are usually not far behind, with the smaller ice usually sticking close to the central hard core of bergs. As these are dragged south each spring by the powerful Labrador Current, the Grand Banks sea-lanes are crossed by massive ice fields, which can be many miles in length and several miles thick. In April in particular, they are a constant menace to sailors. According to the International Ice Patrol, the body set up in the wake of the Titanic disaster, on average about a thousand bergs, plus their numerous ice fields, make the annual migration over this much used strip of sea. After leaving the Grand Banks, the bergs and lesser ice make a slow meandering passage down to the tropics where they finally melt.

Icebergs had been destroying ships ever since man had gone to sea, but smaller ships were perhaps more capable of dealing with them; the incident with the Royal Standard for one thing showed that small steel ships had far more rigidity to their hulls than their larger descendants. Herbert Lightoller in his memoirs recalled that very often the Majestic, when he served aboard her, would strike the wharf a hefty blow, but all that this did was to scratch the paintwork. The same, though to a far lesser extent, was the case with the larger White Star ship, Oceanic.

This opinion is correct; the increasing size of ships and their faster speed did not meet with a revision in the armoured capabilities of the hull. With a far smaller ship, if you were unlucky enough to strike a berg, the chances were that the ship would just bump off it, but with bigger, faster ships, it was a recipe for disaster. Icebergs were not something that could be brushed aside, but increasing advances in the size of ships and their speed seem to have cast a spell over sailors – even Captain Smith with his years of experience seems to have had a naive faith in the impenetrable nature of sheet steel and the power of the mighty turbine, a faith which had tragic results.

However, in 1899, Smith had more pressing matters to concern himself with as the second Boer War started in the British-held Cape Colony. It proved to be a hard-fought campaign between the British army and the smaller, but better armed and far more mobile Boer commandos, and it took two years, close on half a million British troops and several embarrassing defeats before the Boers surrendered. Because of his rank in the Royal Naval Reserve, Smith, along with his ship the Majestic and her crew, was called up for service and had the job of helping to transport the troops to the war zone. Smith and the Majestic made two journeys to South Africa: one to Durban in Natal province and one to Cape Town, the capital of the Colony, which nestled dramatically under the shadow of Table Mountain. These trips were without incident and were merely a variation on transporting normal passengers, but they earned Lieutenant Smith the Transport Medal with the "South Africa" clasp which he ever after wore proudly on his uniform. This was presented to him in 1903 by King Edward VII.

From 1902, with the Boer War virtually won, the steamship companies returned to business as usual, while for Smith it was back to the minor mishaps and accidents in the day-to-day running of a passenger liner. For instance, on 7th April 1901, a bolt fractured in the Majestic's starboard engine and the ship limped along awkwardly on her port engine whilst repairs took place, all of which delayed her arrival in New York by a day. Later that year on 7th August at 5 a.m. a fire broke out in one of the Majestic's linen closets just before the ship reached New York. A hole was made in the deck above the closet and water poured in. However, five hours later there was further smoke coming from the closet, so steam was injected into the recess from the ship's boilers and this remedy worked. The fire, which seems to have been caused by sparks from electrical wires, was apparently not reported to Smith until the voyage was over.

In 1902, the Majestic was ordered to report to Belfast for a refit. There her number of masts was reduced to two. A new mainmast was fitted and the mizzenmast was removed. The refit took some time and it wasn't until 1903 that the Majestic was again ready for service. Therefore, from December 1902 until May 1903, Smith returned to the Germanic.

It was also in 1902 that a happy event occurred when a child was born to Eleanor and Smith, a dark-haired baby girl whom they named Helen Melville Smith. She was to be their only child. The arrival of his daughter seems to have set Smith thinking about what provisions he should make for his family in the event of his death, a possibility that every sailor had to face. To this end, a year after Helen's birth, Smith contacted his solicitor, J.W. Thompson of Liverpool, and had his last will and testament drawn up in full legal fashion. This was signed and witnessed at 17 Marine Crescent, Waterloo, on 11th May 1903. Smith left everything to his wife, with the condition that if she should die or remarry, then the entire property would pass to Helen. The executors of the will were two family friends, David Cooke of 6 Adelaide Terrace, Waterloo, and brewer Thomas Jones of The Nook, Runcorn, Cheshire. Jones seems to have been a very close friend of Smith and had earlier been present at his marriage to Eleanor. The will was then witnessed by Eleanor's sister, Maria, and Thompson, the solicitor.

In May 1903, Smith reassumed command of the Majestic, but in June 1904, after nine long years as her captain, he was taken off the Majestic and given command of White Star's newest vessel, the S.S. Baltic, at that time the largest ship in the world. On 28th June, the day before the Baltic's maiden voyage, Smith indulged the White Star publicity department by giving a newspaper interview. The report went into his career in some detail and it was noted that, 'With his officers he is exceedingly popular.' That a lieutenant, rather than the senior company commander, should have been given the helm of the new 23,000-ton Baltic for her maiden voyage seemed in itself a newsworthy item. The next day, the Baltic under Smith's command set off from Liverpool to New York and arrived there safely several days later after a pleasant and uneventful journey. Looking back over Smith's career, it might be said that when he took command of the new Baltic, his first truly "big ship", he had taken the first step on the ladder that was to lead him to the zenith of his career. The Baltic was, after all, only the first in a series of proposed big ships and Smith was to lead almost all of them out on their maiden voyages.

As the ships grew in size, the excellent deep water harbour of Southampton began to seem a more attractive base of operations for the White Star Line. This inclination grew into a reality in 1907, when Southampton replaced Liverpool as the company's main terminal for transatlantic voyages. Because of this, the Smiths had to move house and they purchased Woodhead, a redbrick, twin-gabled house in Winn Road, in the select Westwood Park district of Southampton.

Although Smith became a member of the executive council of the Mercantile Marine in 1907, family life by then afforded him a pleasant respite. His career was going well, his family was settled and Helen (who for some reason was nicknamed "Babs") was growing up. Shore leave also gave Smith the chance to spend some time with his pet dog, which was a big, white, shaggy Irish wolfhound and there exists a picture of Smith and his dog standing on the deck of one of his ships, possibly the Olympic. Smith was very fond of his pet. The Bishop of Willesden, who became a close friend of Smith, often recalled long evenings talking to him in his cabin, when Smith presented himself as an advanced thinker, but was only too happy to put aside weighty matters to talk lovingly of his family and his pet dog.

There was also the inevitable vice – cigars, which he enjoyed at his leisure. In her later years, his daughter Helen often recalled her father quietly smoking and only allowing her in the room if she kept still and did not disturb the cloud of blue smoke that hung around his head.

Smith still took an interest in the affairs of old friends and in events in his home town. Spencer Till recalled a cordial visit he paid to his friend's home when he was still in Liverpool and Smith made the journey back to the Potteries when he had the time. He never forgot his roots and a few years before the Titanic disaster there was an Etruria British School reunion, planned by some of the old boys and organised so that it would coincide with one of Smith's periods of shore leave. In the event, quite a few turned up, many coming to pay their respects to their old teacher, Alfred Smith, who had long since retired from the school. Spencer Till also attended the get-together and noted that a group photo was taken. Several years later in 1913, Till wrote sadly to Eleanor Smith that seventeen of those in the photograph, including Alfred and Ted Smith, were dead.

Smith left the Baltic in March 1907 and in early May, he possibly assumed brief command of the S.S. Oceanic, a ship widely regarded as the finest in the White Star fleet. She was a one-off, a vessel in her own class with no sister ships and she was generally known as the 'Queen of the Seas'.

However, on 8th May, Smith took command of the new S.S. Adriatic for her maiden voyage. She was his second big ship, eclipsing the Baltic in size. Smith took her out safely and returned her in good order. Whilst in New York, he gave an interview to a reporter from the "New York Times", saying that he had never been in trouble at sea, though like every experienced seaman he had seen his fair share of storms, high seas and fog. The only distressed ship he had ever encountered was a stricken brig, the crew of which had been taken off in a boat by his ship's third officer. He considered his career to have been uneventful and as he had avoided danger thus far, he was unable to foresee any in the future and was reported as saying with some confidence that, 'Modern shipbuilding has gone beyond that.'

This may have been a representative instance of a good P.R. man doing his job, but it was also a rather rash statement. Of all his reported speech this is perhaps the statement that seems to show a streak of blatant overconfidence in Smith's attitude to his job, a feeling that nothing could go wrong. There were some later stories reporting that perhaps he was not as confident in the safety of his ships, especially regarding the provision of lifeboats (aboard the Olympic), but these stories are apocryphal, and it seems highly unlikely that a man in his position would voice such doubts to the passengers, even if he had misgivings. Yet overconfidence was an attitude that White Star's own regulations cautioned against; regulation no. 2 in the ship's rules that hung conspicuously on every White Star bridge read, 'Overconfidence – a most fruitful source of accidents, should be especially guarded against.' The problem area in the interpretation of such rules, though, was how far complete adherence to them would affect a ship's performance and the company's popularity. Were the ethics of big business outstripping the ethics of safety?

Smith's statement appears all the more ironic, as it was with the Adriatic that cracks in the veneer of the White Star company's image began to show. On 10th October 1908, four crewmen were charged with looting passengers' luggage and hoards of stolen property, to the value of $15,000, were found hidden around the ship. Almost two years later on 8th August 1910, the ship's firemen mutinied whilst she was in Southampton. It is prudent not to over-emphasize these events, as they were not the footsteps of doom chasing after Captain Smith, but were merely minor troubles which were soon resolved. Only with hindsight do these experiences on the Adriatic, and presently on the Olympic, seem to show fate building up to something disastrous with which to end Smith's relatively blameless career.

In 1907, the White Star chairman, J. Bruce Ismay, the son of the late Thomas Henry Ismay, met with Lord William Pirrie, the chairman of Harland and Wolff shipyard, to discuss a pet project, the results of which, by 1910, were nearing the first stages of completion. In 1907, the new and very fast Cunard liners, Lusitania and Mauretania, had suddenly appeared on the shipping scene. Ismay was sensible to the fact that any new vessels built for White Star had to come close to matching these Cunard greyhounds if the company wanted to keep a firm hold on its share of the market. Yet to Ismay's mind, this increase in speed did not mean a decrease in the high degree of luxury afforded by White Star ships. To this end he had conceived a project for the building of three big ships, each nearly twice the size of the Baltic or the Adriatic, to take over as their first-class Royal Mail ships operating the prestigious Southampton to New York route. The vessels, to be over 40,000 tons each, were given the names Olympic, Titanic and Gigantic (though the Gigantic was later renamed Britannic after the Titanic disaster, as White Star did not like to tempt fate with a name so similar to that of the Titanic). They were to be ships whose very names pointed to their colossal sizes. Within two years of this meeting, the keels of the Olympic and the Titanic had been laid down at Harland and Wolff. Over a year after that, the Olympic was launched and on 31st May 1911, she became the property of the White Star Line.

Like her sister after her, at her launch the R.M.S. Olympic was the largest ship in the world. In her first-class accommodation she was sumptuous beyond belief, whilst her second and third-class facilities far exceeded the norm in passenger comforts. The Olympic was 882 feet long, weighed 45,324 tons, had three propellers and four huge funnels, and, like the Titanic after her, incorporated the same safety factors – sixteen compartments divided by fifteen watertight bulkheads. The ship's safety factors were discussed a great deal before her launch; as it was, they not only far exceeded the necessary British safety regulations of the time, but even outstripped modern-day regulations. Yet for some reason the Olympic excited far less interest from the press than the Titanic would later enjoy, and there was no open talk of her being unsinkable, despite a White Star flyer describing her as such. The Olympic was merely considered to be very safe and reliable.

Since the start of his time in command of the Adriatic, Smith had been promoted and honoured and was by 1911 Commander Edward John Smith R.D., R.N.R., a Reserve Decoration having been added after his name on account of his receipt in 1910 of the R.N.R. Long Service Medal, which he now wore with his Boer War decoration. He was by then a stocky, white-bearded, genial sexagenarian, liked by his crew and passengers and trusted by his employers. There had been a few hiccups with the Adriatic, but nothing that detracted from his reputation as a first-rate liner captain. On the company payroll, the only other man with Smith's record of service was Commander Herbert J. Haddock. However, since the launch of the Baltic in 1904, Smith had been the man entrusted with taking the new ships out on their first run and so he was given command of the massive new Olympic.

Before taking the helm of the Olympic, Smith found time to make a trip to the Potteries on a visit to family and friends. For a while he stayed with his nephew, J.W.S. Harrington, who had by then retired from the sea, married, set up home in Hanley and was working as a builder. Evidently Smith was pleased at having been given command of the Olympic and talked confidently about the strengths of the new vessel. Mrs. Harrington heard him say words to the effect that the Olympic, 'was firm as a church'.

Under Smith's command, the Olympic left Southampton on her maiden voyage on 11th June 1911 and her journey to the United States was quiet and uneventful. The Olympic became a popular ship and was the only one of the big ships commissioned to reach the breaker's yard after a lifetime of near sterling service. Liked by both crew and passengers, she justly earned the nickname "Old Reliable".

However, in what was to follow, it seemed that the Olympic was giving a foretaste of what was to come. Her maiden voyage ended on 21st June, when the ship steamed slowly into New York Harbour. The liner was then docked at pier 59 and twelve tugs were gently easing her into position when the first accident of her career occurred. One of the tugs, the 198-ton O.L. Halenbeck, suddenly found herself caught in the backwash from the ship's starboard propeller, which span the tug around and trapped her under the stern of the liner. The tug's ensign mast splintered like matchwood against the Olympic's overhanging stern and the smaller vessel span away until she found herself stuck against an underwater cable that dragged her down by the bow until her decks were awash and she seemed in danger of sinking. However, as an anxious crowd gathered to watch, the O.L. Halenbeck somehow managed to get her mangled frame out of the wash and away from the cable, and struggled over to a nearby pier.

This was the first in a series of potentially dangerous accidents involving the Olympic and the Titanic, all of which, barring the Titanic's fatal collision, happened within confined harbours or estuaries and seemed to have their bases in the fact that the men in charge of the vessels were inexperienced in handling ships of the bulk of the Olympic-class liners and were ignorant of the hydrodynamic forces such vessels caused around them. Although the main force on the O.L. Halenbeck had been from the Olympic's propeller, the inexperience of even the most timeserved seaman in operating a big ship in confined waters was amply borne out by the

Olympic's most notable mishap, when she was involved in a collision with the Royal Navy cruiser H.M.S. Hawke.

On 20th September 1911, the Olympic set off on her fifth transatlantic voyage, leaving the White Star dock in Southampton at 11.20 a.m. Southampton's port regulations required a pilot on the bridge until the vessel reached the open sea and under Smith's watchful gaze, the Trinity House harbour pilot, "Uncle" George Bowyer, guided the ship down Southampton Water. Where Southampton Water meets the Isle of Wight, the pilot had the choice of two routes out into the English Channel: either to starboard down the Solent, or to port following the intricate Spithead passage around a large shoal known as "Bramble Bank". The latter was Smith's favourite route out into the English Channel and the Olympic turned to port and began cruising along at about 17 knots, though the speed was reduced as the ship neared the Bramble. At 12.40, with her speed then down to 11 knots and approaching the most difficult part of the manoeuvre, the Olympic's whistles were sounded twice, signalling to other shipping that she was attempting a port turn. It was about then that several of the ship's officers noticed a naval vessel coming up behind the Olympic, two miles off the starboard quarter. This ship was the cruiser, H.M.S. Hawke.

Having completed her manoeuvre, the Olympic, then powering up, was still some distance ahead of the Hawke, but presently the cruiser began to draw up to her and was soon running on a parallel course to the Olympic, about 600 feet away on the starboard side. Bowyer was certain that when the Olympic was opened up the Hawke would drop back and sure enough, as the liner's speed increased, the cruiser, which had been on a line with the Olympic's bridge, began to be outpaced. It seems to have been the intention of the Hawke's captain to drop in behind the stern of the Olympic, as the liner was to his mind the overtaking vessel. A slight turn to port would have facilitated this, but suddenly the Hawke, having reached a point level with the centre of the Olympic, took a sharp turn to port that threw those on the Olympic's bridge into a panic.

'I don't believe he will get under our stern, Bowyer,' said Smith, alarmed by the move.

'If she's going to strike, sir, let me know in time so I can put the helm hard over to port,' said Bowyer, who then shouted, 'Is she going to strike, sir?'

'Yes, she is going to strike us in the stern,' Smith called back.

Bowyer put the helm hard over and the ship began to turn, but it was all too late and the ramnose of the Hawke crunched into the Olympic's stern, leaving a fifteen-feet long triangular-shaped hole in the liner and a crack that reached below the water line. The emergency doors separating the watertight compartments were immediately closed and Bowyer stopped the engines. The extensive damage to the White Star vessel brought her journey to an abrupt end. The Olympic was unable to return to port until the next high tide, so Smith and Bowyer anchored her for the night in Osborne Bay off Cowes on the Isle of Wight. There, the passengers were taken off by a tender and returned to Southampton where they had to make other travel arrangements. The next morning the Olympic was tugged back to the docks and once she was berthed, her cargos were off-loaded, while at the same time a party of divers and White Star officials took a look at the damage incurred. They decided that it was enough to require dry-docking and the only facilities large enough for this were the Belfast yards where the ship had been built. However, before the ship could even contemplate the 600-mile trip to Belfast, she had to be given a temporary patch; steel plates were fixed beneath the water line and the large hole above the water was patched with wood.

The other protagonist, H.M.S. Hawke, listed to the nose and only stayed afloat through vigorous pumping. The Hawke limped back to Portsmouth for repairs that took ten months. The only good thing about the entire incident was that nobody had been hurt.

It took more than ten days for the temporary repairs to the Olympic to be completed. Smith went home, but on 22nd September was in front of Alexander Paris, a public notary of Southampton, to whom he outlined, in the insurance protest, his version of events. Paris noted down that the Olympic,

'at 12.46 p.m. while proceeding to Spithead was run into by H.M.S. Hawke causing serious damage which compelled him

[Smith] to anchor, and subsequently, namely at 8 a.m. on the twenty-first day of September, returned to Southampton Docks, where the vessel arrived at 10.30 a.m. the same day.'

It seemed a clear-cut case of bad manoeuvring on the part of the Hawke's captain and there was little reason to doubt that the Royal Navy would be footing the White Star repair bill. However, when the whole matter was brought to an inquiry, things did not turn out as expected.

White Star immediately sued the Admiralty and the Hawke's captain, Commander William Blunt, but this was soon countered by an Admiralty action for the damage done to the Hawke, which was in the process of having 20 feet of her bow amputated. The inquiry into the events of 20th September began on 16th November 1911, aboard the warship Duke of Wellington at anchor in Portsmouth. The commanders of both the vessels involved, as well as Pilot Bowyer, were brought in to testify, with each in turn presenting his evidence. Commander Blunt made it clear that he felt that the manoeuvre he had made at 600 feet distant from the Olympic had been by far enough to take his ship behind the overtaking Olympic. White Star claimed that the navy had been careless, while the navy argued that the Olympic had gone too close to the Hawke, but there was another explanation laid before the Admiralty court which was the more likely cause of the collision.

George Baker, an official from the National Physical Laboratory, was brought in to testify that the two vessels had in fact been the victims of a strange suction which occurred between them. The theory was then novel, but nowadays it is a well-accepted fact in the science of physics that all vessels, whether cruising in air or in water, produce a fluctuating series of fields of pressure around them as they move. The heavier the vessel's bulk, the greater these pressures become, as too is the effect that they have on neighbouring craft. Increased pressure from the bow and stern of a ship and decreased pressure from the middle therefore cause forces of repulsion and attraction strong enough to throw the lesser vessels around as if they are rag dolls. Mr. Baker put it like this:

'When one vessel overtakes another and is so placed that the bows feel the power of the reduced pressure and the stern is in the field of the increased pressure, the bow will turn in and the stern will move out.'

This was exactly the position that the Hawke found herself in in relation to the Olympic when she executed her sudden and unexpected turn. These forces had always existed, but it was only in the early years of the twentieth century, with the advent of the big ships, that these formerly little-noticed forces became a positive menace to shipping. Such hydrodynamics later played a part in the near collision between the Titanic and another vessel during the start of the Titanic's fateful voyage.

The verdict of the Admiralty court, however, did not agree with Baker's explanation. On 19th December, Sir Samuel Adams for the Admiralty decided that the Olympic alone was to blame, the cause being negligent navigation on the part of Pilot Bowyer. It was a verdict that saved White Star pride, as the accident had taken place under compulsory pilotage, but it was not the outcome they had looked for. Nor was Smith pleased and he wrote stiffly to a friend that, 'we are not taking it lying down'. As expected, White Star lodged an appeal. This was a lengthy affair and reached its conclusion long after Smith himself was dead. On 5th April 1913, the Admiralty verdict was upheld and the White Star appeal was dismissed with costs.

In retrospect, some see this as having been another ill omen regarding Captain Smith. Despite the fact that Bowyer had been in compulsory command of the Olympic, people noted that Smith was the captain, who years earlier had said, 'I never saw a wreck and have never been wrecked, nor was I ever in any predicament that threatened to end in disaster of any sort.' This incident could have been disastrous, and indeed would have been had not the passengers whose cabins were destroyed been at lunch with the rest of those on board at the time. It seemed that Smith may have "broken his luck" with the Olympic-Hawke collision. However, in the event, the court's verdict did not affect the careers of any of those involved in the incident, as Commander Blunt was promoted to captain, George Bowyer continued to work as a Southampton harbour pilot and Smith shortly rose to the status of the White Star

Line's most experienced commander and earned the title "Commodore of the Fleet".

Meanwhile, the Olympic underwent repairs in dry dock, reconstruction work that cost about £103,000. Interestingly, as if fate were at work, the repairs to the Olympic, especially the purloining of one of the Titanic's propellers to replace one damaged in the collision, bumped the Titanic's start date for her maiden voyage from 20th March 1912 to 10th April.

The journey cancelled after the Hawke incident took place on 30th November 1911 and, despite a delayed start due to fog, was quiet and uninterrupted. So too were the Olympic's subsequent voyages in 1911. In January 1912, the ship ran into snow and towering seas that surprised Smith with their ferocity. Waves dashed against and over the Olympic. One large wave lifted the ship's bow clear of the water and just as she settled down into a trough, another wave crashed down on her, ripping off a hatch cover and smashing some of the deck machinery. However, the ship got safely through that journey. Then in February 1912, the Olympic dropped a propeller when she ran over what appeared to be a sunken wreck, but these were run-of-the-mill incidents that afforded the sorts of bumps and scrapes that most busy ships could expect in their terms of service.

One thing still left undamaged by any of these mishaps, though, was the standing of Smith in the eyes of his employers. He was by then the highest paid man at sea, earning £1,250 a year plus an extra thousand if he returned his ships in good order. During his long career, he was reckoned to have commanded seventeen ships and it was estimated that he had clocked up over 2,000,000 miles on his travels. He was also the senior commander of the White Star Line, but more than that he was the epitome of confidence and safety on the high seas, the unsinkable Captain Smith – at least that was how it seemed. He was a man prepared to stake his life on the quality of the service he offered and the ships he commanded. There is an unsubstantiated story that a fortune-teller had predicted that the 'largest liner in the world' would sink in 1912. At the time Smith heard of this prediction he was still the commander of the Olympic which was still the largest liner in the world. In answer to the tale

Smith is supposed to have replied unequivocally, 'If the largest ship in the world sinks, I will go down with her.' In an old newsreel that showed him walking around on one of his ships, his confidence shone through, and he appeared as Herbert Lightoller saw him, as the 'beau ideal of a western ocean mail boat captain'.

White Star probably bore all of these factors in mind when they chose him to command their latest ship. Smith was by then 62 years old; stories have it that he was due for retirement after the next journey, though such a valuable asset as Smith may well have been kept on until the third Olympic-class liner came into service, making a hat trick with which he could round off his career. Certainly, though, White Star could not conceive of anyone more capable of taking command of the second of their great liners, a ship that was already receiving massive press attention – the newest, largest, most luxurious ship in the world ... R.M.S. Titanic.

4
Futility

In the years since the sinking of the Titanic, many legends and stories have built up around the disaster, for instance, the famous story that the ship was 'unsinkable' and the false legend that the Titanic was the largest liner that has ever been built (the Q.E.2 is nearly 1,000 feet long, compared with the Titanic, which was 882 feet, and the Q.E.2 is about 20,000 tons heavier). Later we will also see how many stories have originated as to how Captain Smith met his end.

Other intriguing tales surrounding the disaster are the many 'what-if' situations that occurred on the night in question, but even more interesting are some of the stories that were written well before the Titanic was even conceived – tales that bear uncanny resemblance to fact. As well as the stories written by the journalist W.T. Stead, there is one more tale, so startling in its similarities to the disaster that was to overtake the Titanic that it deserves to be told in some detail.

It was in 1898 that an American author, a former merchant navy officer named Morgan Robertson, wrote a short novel entitled "Futility". The book was not a best seller by any means, nor has memory of the story survived because it attracted a great deal of critical acclaim as a work of art. Robertson wrote many novels, a number of which were concerned with the sea, and they have all vanished into obscurity, as no doubt "Futility" would have done had not Robertson predicted with uncanny accuracy within its pages events that were not to happen for fourteen years.

"Futility" described the maiden voyage of the largest ship afloat, a British liner of unparalleled luxury. The ship displaced 70,000 tons fully laden and was over 800 feet long. She had three propellers driven by three triple expansion reciprocating engines that could produce a top speed of 24 to 25 knots. She was subdivided by 19 watertight bulkheads, a facility that made her designers consider her unsinkable. The ship could carry a maximum of 3,000 people, though for the maiden voyage there were only 2,000 on board. Even so, this was 1,500 more than could be safely accommodated in her 24 lifeboats.

Robertson's fictional ship set sail in April from Southampton to New York and to increase the ship's speed for a record crossing, the crew hoisted gigantic triangular sails to help her along. So impetuous was this journey that when the liner ran down and sank a small windjammer, the crew did not stop to pick up the survivors out of the water, one of whom shouted a curse at the ship as she sped on. This curse caught up with the ship in mid-Atlantic when on a foggy but moonlit night, the ship struck an iceberg on its starboard side, slid up a slope of ice and reared out of the water, tilting drunkenly over to starboard as she did so. Because of the impact, her engines broke from their mountings and smashed into the hull, holing the ship. Then the vessel slid back down the iceberg, an action which smashed up her starboard boats, before she settled back in the calm sea, where she endured a lingering death from which there were only thirteen survivors. The name of Robertson's fictional ship was S.S. Titan.

Ever since the Titanic disaster plucked Robertson's book back from the edge of oblivion, many people have been amazed at the similarities between the fate of the fictional Titan and the real-life Titanic. Their comparative sizes, capacities, types of engine (the Titanic had two triple expansion reciprocating engines and a single steam turbine engine), their lack of lifeboats, their transverse bulkheads and especially their names and the fates that awaited them on their maiden voyages have led many to believe that Robertson had exhibited one of those rare instances of second sight or precognition. What little is known about Morgan Robertson seems to support this idea, as the novelist was something of a spiritualist, who claimed that his stories were dictated to him from an astral writing partner. Other people, such as George Behe, the author of "Titanic: Psychic Forewarnings of a Tragedy", take the alternative view that rather than being influenced by a partner on another astral plane, Robertson constructed his story from his long association with ships and shipping lore and made a shrewd deduction of the dangers and futility (as the book's title implied) that faulty maritime practice could result in.

There are, of course, differences in the two tales: the Titan's use of sail to aid its record crossing was an idea dating back to the early days of steam shipping when Robertson was at sea. The Titanic did not use sails and, despite stories to the contrary, she was not after a record crossing, because she was incapable of such; the speedy Cunarders had her beaten hands down. The Titan struck the iceberg and suffered some damage, but most of her damage came from the impact of her own machinery, whereas the Titanic was damaged by the iceberg alone. The Titan's starboard boats were smashed up, whereas all of the Titanic's left the ship safely; only 13 people survived the sinking of the Titan, but there were 705 rescued from the Titanic. Yet, for all of this, Robertson's clear-minded prediction of disaster still remains fresh and startling in its reasoning of what could and would happen if man's confidence in his inventions and the powers of his technology grew to know no bounds.

Fourteen years later, Robertson's fiction became a reality.

5

Titanic

The keel of what was to become the great ship, Titanic, had been laid down in Harland and Wolff shipyard in 1909 and the shell of the ship, minus her upper works and imposing funnels, was launched on 31st May 1911. There was no naming ceremony for the ship, as depicted in the film "A Night To Remember", because the White Star company did not believe in such events. The ship was merely launched down the slipway, thrilling the spectators as she glided down to the water, helped on her way by tons of grease and soft soap, and dragged piles of chains with her to slow the release. Among the spectators over whom the ship was to gain a hold, was a young Irish lad named William McQuitty. In later life he became a respected film producer and was the driving force behind "A Night To Remember".

For the rest of that year, the Titanic underwent further construction. Each morning, the welders, fitters, carpenters and other workers arrived in their hundreds through the factory gates, nearly all clad in a similar fashion, with rough work clothes and the ubiquitous flat cap. All converged on the gigantic form that was gradually taking shape on the wharf. For some, there was a temporary diversion to the repair work that needed to be done to the Olympic, which was moored in the adjacent quay after her brush with H.M.S. Hawke. Soon the Titanic assumed her full shape, needing only a lick of paint.

She was painted in the traditional White Star colours. The hull was painted red below the water line and black above, though the edges of the forecastle and poop deck were painted white, as were the rest of the upper works. At the top of the hull was a mark of the line's quality – a thin gold band that ran around the ship. The funnels were buff yellow topped with black, the masts were brown topped with a teak pole and the decks were of polished planking. Hatch covers and some of the bases beneath the funnels were grey and capstans gleamed of bronze, while ventilator cones were white with red innards. Everything was neat and functional and once in service it was kept spotlessly clean. The final touch was the name "TITANIC", painted on either side of the bow and "TITANIC/ LIVERPOOL" (underneath) on the stern.

The vital statistics of the ship were most people's talking points; in overall length the Titanic measured 882 feet 9 inches, she was 92 feet wide and 104 feet from keel to bridge. Period newspapers made efforts to convey the size of the ship in more visible terms, placing a drawing of the ship amidst the buildings of central London in one, or putting her on end against the Eiffel Tower and the Pyramids in another. In gross tonnage, the Titanic weighed 46, 328 tons, over 1,000 tons heavier than the Olympic, and she displaced an estimated 60,000 tons in the water. The ship had accommodation for 3,547 people: 905 in first class, 564 in second, 1,134 in third class and accommodation for a crew of 944.

The engines were studied in detail. Motive power, up to an estimated top speed of 24 to 25 knots, came from the latest thing in maritime engineering: two triple expansion engines to power the ship's wing propellers and a smaller turbine engine for the central propeller. These were fed by 29 truly monstrous boilers, which were arranged in rows through six separate compartments amidships. The boilers also supplied the heating for the ship's massive plumbing system, not only to the cabins but also to the galleys, the ship's swimming bath and the elegant first-class saunas and Turkish baths.

There were sporting facilities: a squash court on G deck and a fully equipped gymnasium on A deck. Both came with their own professional instructor. The ship's restaurants were extensive; the first-class à la carte restaurant was carpeted throughout, unlike on the Olympic, and afforded the last word in elegance. The facilities for second and third class, though less elegant, were considered the best on any ship afloat.

But the greatest luxury undoubtedly went into the cabins. For those in second or third class, the cabins were essentially utilitarian, very similar to what we expect today, but in first class, especially for those in the most expensive staterooms, comfort, luxury and sheer unadulterated elegance were the watchwords. Rooms were decorated with panelling and stucco, Adam fireplaces with real coal fires, Regency furniture and Minton, Royal Doulton and the finest Wedgwood porcelain. All sorts of tastes and architectural styles were catered for, with Dutch, Queen Anne, Elizabethan, Louis V, Adam, Regency, Georgian and more contemporary designs. Some staterooms housed four-poster beds, tapestries hung across the walls and beautiful Limoges glassware decorated the rooms, along with ornate mirrors, splendid Chesterfields or reproduction Chippendales. The decoration was limited only, perhaps, by the creativity of the various craftsmen employed in producing such beautiful settings. The two most spendid staterooms on board were each fifty feet long and had their own enclosed promenade deck, but these were affordable only by those in the millionaire class.

The menus aboard such a luxury vessel were something to be savoured. Given notice, almost anything could be provided from the ship's extensive store of provisions. The surviving copy of the Titanic's cargo manifest shows the stores she carried for her maiden voyage. These included 75,000lbs of fresh meat, 25,000lbs of poultry, 11,000lbs of fresh fish, 4,000lbs of salted and dried fish, 1,500 gallons of fresh milk, 6,000lbs of butter, 10,000lbs of cereals, 40 tons of potatoes, 50 boxes of grapefruit, 2,200lbs of coffee, 1,000lbs of tea, 15,000 bottles of ale and stout, 1,000 bottles of wine and 8,000 cigars!

The Titanic incorporated the latest safety features. Inside her hull, she was subdivided by 15 watertight transverse bulkheads, making 16 separate compartments. These were interconnected by a series of emergency watertight doors that in the event of flooding could be closed either singly by the engineer on the spot, or all of them automatically from the bridge by a small switch. The hull itself was double-bottomed, with a secondary hull built inside the main hull. If the main hull of one-inch thick plate steel was breached, the designers were confident that the secondary hull would hold. The space in between these two hulls was approximately seven feet, easy enough for a man to walk through.

TITANIC

Yet given all of these features, did the designers say that the ship was unsinkable? Of all the great legends surrounding the Titanic, the story that the ship was said to be 'unsinkable' has been the most enduring and the most ironic in the light of what was to happen to her on her first outing. Sir Philip Gibbs in his contemporary work, "The Deathless Story of the Titanic", quotes White Star publicity as having said that the ship was unsinkable. The company did say this, albeit in a qualified manner. In 1911, White Star issued a small four-page publicity leaflet showing the two sisters, the Olympic and the Titanic, on the stocks at Harland and Wolff, accompanied by an artist's impression of how they would look when they were finished. The leaflets went on to describe the dimensions, weight and luxurious appointments of the two liners. Then, in the final paragraph came the fatal phrase, '. . . and as far as it is possible to do so, these two wonderful vessels are designed to be unsinkable.' These leaflets seem to have been intended for shipping offices and travel agents, but the vast majority were quietly withdrawn and destroyed after the Titanic disaster made their existence highly embarrassing.

Another source of the unsinkable legend was a contemporary shipping journal that reviewed the Titanic and described her as 'practically unsinkable', but it may have been echoing White Star's own generalisation. Certainly, by the time the Titanic set sail, many of the passengers had the spurious notion in their heads that the ship could not sink; this caused many to delay when disaster struck and cost them their lives.

Then there were the lifeboats. Though the in-built safety factors were ahead of their time, it emerges as something rather sad in the reasoning of big businessmen that they should deliberately skimp on the simplest of safety equipment, the humble lifeboat. Their neglect was compounded to some extent by the fact that the big ships of the early twentieth century had rapidly outstripped existing maritime legislation regarding the provision of lifeboats. By 1912, the British Board of Trade's laws in this respect were hopelessly outdated and held that vessels exceeding 10,000 tons were only legally required to carry 16 lifeboats, irrespective of how many people were on board. Originally, the designers of the Titanic had planned for the ship to carry 32 lifeboats, for well over 2,000 people, but in the event, the company decided that it could do without the extra expense that 16 more lifeboats would create – besides, the ship was safe enough with her in-built safety features and too many lifeboats along the deck spoilt the view! So the Titanic received only the necessary 16 lifeboats, ranged eight either side of the ship, slung from Welin davits. As a rather ironic gesture, the company provided the ship with four Engelhardt collapsible lifeboats; these were wooden-keeled, canvas-sided craft, which were flimsy but perfectly seaworthy and White Star felt that they would give the ship that extra edge of safety. They were lashed in place on the roof of the officers' quarters.

Emphasis was also placed on the extra safety provided via the Marconi telegraph system that the new liner was to carry. The wireless had a little room of its own situated not far behind the bridge. From there the two wireless operators that the Titanic was to carry could keep a 24-hour watch. The system operated between receiving stations in both Britain and America and messages could be relayed between ships via their own shorter-range transmitters. The Titanic's aerial was strung out between her two masts and hummed and crackled, much to the interest of the passengers when they came on board.

In early 1912, the Titanic underwent her speed trials after taking on board her complement of officers, as well as Captain Smith. With a skeleton crew on board, the new ship was put through her paces in a nearby stretch of water in sight of her Belfast yards. The tests consisted of a set of standard manoeuvres designed to satisfy Board of Trade inspectors of the ship's seaworthiness. The Titanic had been inspected on about 2,000 separate occasions during her construction, all of which culminated with these trials. Interestingly enough, whilst in Belfast Lough, the Titanic was made to execute a manoeuvre that she was later to repeat, though with less satis-factory results than then. Cruising along at about 20 knots, the helm was put hard over to starboard and the engines reversed. This was to test the reaction of the ship to the wheel, her turning circle and her stopping distance. The ship came to a dead stop in 850 yards in just over half a minute. The inspectors were satisfied with the ship's performance.

Once the trials were out of the way, the Titanic was handed over officially to her owners, White Star. The ship cruised steadily from Belfast until she reached Southampton on 2nd April, where she was filled with coal. Provisions began to come aboard and final arrangements made ready for the vessel's maiden voyage. The arrival of the new White Star giant was welcomed in Southampton as an extra source of work for the large seafaring community. Smith, though, had a week to spare before he was due to set sail, so he returned home to Winn Road.

Wednesday 10th April 1912, the sailing day, was fresh and clear when it arrived. Smith left Woodhead shortly before 7 a.m. and got into a waiting taxi, from which he exchanged a final wave with Eleanor and Helen. From his home in Winn Road, the taxi took him through the centre of Southampton before going down the hill towards the docks, where the mighty Titanic loomed large against the other vessels moored there.

He boarded the Titanic at about 7.30 and went straight to his cabin, where he changed out of his civilian bowler hat and over-coat and donned his uniform. This consisted of a pair of dark blue trousers and a long, dark blue double-breasted jacket, with four gold rings on each cuff denoting his command rank. Last of all was the blue peaked cap bearing the laurels, crown and red pennant badge of the White Star Line. There followed immediately after this a meeting with the Titanic's chief officer, Henry Wilde, who brought the sailing report to the captain's cabin. Wilde had been Smith's chief officer on the Olympic and had been transferred to the new liner at Smith's personal request, a move that bumped a number of the Titanic's other officers down a rung. Wilde, a trusted and professional officer in the execution of his duties, had, like many of the other officers, spent the night on board getting to know the new vessel.

Captain Clarke, the Board of Trade immigration officer, also came aboard the Titanic at about 7.30 a.m. He made his final inspection of the ship, then he and Smith spent the morning signing and countersigning final reports before sailing. During this time, the Titanic's crew had begun to arrive – over 900 people of both sexes and of varying ages and seagoing experience. About 340 of these were such people as the engineers, boilermen, trimmers and firemen who worked below decks and were seldom seen by the passengers. Their experience of any journey took place in often cramped, noisy conditions and in a hothouse atmosphere far removed from the luxuries enjoyed by the passengers. Another 290 crew members were stewards and stewardesses, who attended to the needs of the passengers. The rest were miscellaneous workers, such as pantrymen, P.T. instructors, waiters, cooks, bakers and a masseur. There was also the ship's small professional band, whose members were the pick of the musicians employed by White Star or poached from other shipping companies. All of these took a while to come on board, but as soon as they had, muster lists were taken, which were eventually handed over to Captain Clarke before he left.

The muster and roll call started at 8 a.m. and took an hour to complete. John Podesta, one of the ship's many firemen, arrived in time and was signed on for the journey. Then, as the ship was not due to sail until noon, like most of the other firemen and trimmers, he went ashore, accompanied by some of his friends from the 4 to 8 watch. Podesta and a friend of his, named William Nutbean, went to a local pub, the Newcastle Hotel, before moving onto the Grapes where they met several others and they stayed there until they returned to the ship at 11.50.

One man who may not have had a chance to go ashore for a last few hours was the fourth senior engineer, Leonard Hodgkinson. He was 45 years old, married with three children and lived in Arthur Road, Liverpool. Like the ship's captain he had been born in the Potteries, at 20 North Street, Stoke, and he was the fifth child and second son of pottery presser, John Hodgkinson, and his wife Caroline. Leonard had been educated at St. Thomas' School, Stoke, and when he left had been apprenticed to Messrs. Hartley and Arnoux, whose works were later carried on by Messrs. Kerr, Stuart and Co. Later, he had taken a position with Messrs. Lairds of Birkenhead and subsequently had become a marine engineer. By 1912, he had been with White Star for several years and had served aboard the Celtic and the Olympic, having been aboard the latter during her collision with H.M.S. Hawke. He still had many relatives living in the Potteries; his mother was resident in Shelton Old Road, Stoke, while his younger brother Laurence lived in Seaford Street, Shelton, and worked at Sherratts outfitters in Piccadilly, Hanley.

As one of the engineers under the command of the Titanic's chief engineer, Joseph Bell, it is unlikely that Leonard Hodgkinson had any direct contact with Captain Smith other than on a professional basis and it seems equally unlikely that they realised that they shared a similar background. Certainly, once aboard the ship, these two officers of the Titanic moved in separate worlds and while Smith calmly walked his bridge or the scrubbed-clean upper decks, or spent time talking to the passengers, Hodgkinson and his fellow engineers lived in an enclosed world, fussing over their noisy engines with only the rarest view of sea or sky.

As the crew muster rolls were taken, the ship's officers gathered on the bridge, where each in turn submitted his sectional reports to Chief Officer Wilde. Having read the reports, Wilde deemed the ship to be ready for sea and informed the captain. Also ready by then were the first and second-class passenger lists, copies of which were handed over to Smith who studied them with some interest. The first-class list in particular contained an impressive cross section of rich, famous, landed and titled men and women from both sides of the Atlantic. Together they formed a microcosm of the cream of transatlantic society. The ship carried four multi-millionaires, all of them Americans: Colonel J.J. Astor, who was worth about £30,000,000; Benjamin Guggenheim, who owned £20,000,000 and Isidor Straus, the owner of the famous Macy chain of stores, and George Widener, who were both worth about £10,000,000. A few other passengers were listed as being worth between £1,000,000 and £5,000,000. There were members of the British nobility, such as the Countess of Rothes and Lord and Lady Cosmo Duff Gordon; emissaries, such as Major Archibald Butt, the close friend and personal aide to President Taft of the U.S.A.; influential reporters, such as W.T. Stead, who years earlier had written those prophetic tales of Atlantic disaster; sports stars, such as the tennis player Karl H. Behr, and a whole host of society notables, beauties, doctors, old soldiers and suchlike.

First class also carried a few guest passengers for this maiden journey, one being J. Bruce Ismay, the chairman of the White Star Line, who had originally envisaged the Olympic-class liners. If Ismay represented the Titanic in concept, then another first-class passenger, Thomas Andrews, the managing director of Harland and Wolff, represented the realisation of Ismay's dream, since Andrews had been one of the principal designers of the ship, and at the head of a small team had joined the Titanic for her maiden voyage to see how well she ran.

These passengers were among the first to arrive aboard the ship that morning. Next came the second-class passengers. One of these was Lawrence Beesley, a young schoolmaster from Dulwich College, who planned to tour the States. He had decided to make the crossing aboard the Titanic because of the novelty of being a passenger on the largest ship in the world. He had relied on the reports of friends who had journeyed on board the Olympic, which they had found to be very comfortable and so Beesley was intent on discovering how the Titanic fared in this respect.

He had stayed the night in town and had sat that morning in a breakfast room from the window of which could be seen the four huge funnels of the Titanic, towering over the roofs and other shipping. Behind him had sat three other passengers, discussing the ship and estimating among other things the likelihood of an accident at sea.

Beesley went aboard ship at 10 a.m. and before sailing, he and a group of friends from Exeter explored the various decks, the dining rooms and the libraries, which they found to be very impressive. On their tour, they also wandered into the gymnasium with its various weird and wonderful exercise machines under the charge of the energetic T.W. McCawley, the ship's professional P.T. instructor. He was showing off the equipment to press photographers and putting through their paces a number of volunteer guinea pigs, who were jiggled about, much to the amusement of the press and the crowd of onlookers.

Meanwhile, between 9.30 and 11 a.m., the third-class passengers came aboard the Titanic in crowds. By 11 o'clock, George Bowyer, the Trinity House harbour pilot, had boarded and he spent much of the morning discussing draught and displacement and turning circles with Smith. It was, after all, fewer than eight months since his embarrassing encounter with H.M.S. Hawke and he had no wish to repeat the incident, least of all with White Star's new flagship.

The whistles were blown for all ashore for non-passengers and Lawrence Beesley parted with his friends, as did hundreds of others. When the visitors had gone, the gangplanks were drawn in. Eventually, when everything was ready, with documents all signed, the crew working, the passengers accommodated and the engines fired, Smith, with perhaps a brief smile playing on his face, ordered a quartermaster to sound the whistles for departure. Three triple-tone hoots rang out loud over Southampton Harbour, followed by a further trio once the blue peter had been run up the mast. Pilot Bowyer ordered tugs in to make fast forward and aft and as the powerful little boats took the strain, dwarfed under the immense bulk of the Titanic, the quayside mooring lines were cast off and as they splashed into the water were hauled aboard the ship by her crew. Slowly and carefully, the tugs eased the liner down the River Test towards her turning circle and once there, on Bowyer's command, manoeuvred the ship to the correct position for her departure. Then and only then, did the tug lines slacken and fall, and the Titanic's propellers slowly began to spin.

All this was accompanied by final farewells and shouted last messages from the crowd of friends and relatives who had followed the Titanic along the quayside. None of the other ships paid any attention, though – there was no sounding of whistles or any other overt display, as might have been expected for the maiden voyage of such a grand liner, and the Titanic slipped from her quay as if it were just an ordinary working day.

The ship's telegraph jangled to 'Ahead slow', and followed by final goodbyes shouted over the intervening ships, the Titanic increased her speed marginally, cruising forward past the docks and the numerous ships that remained tied up there. Two of these were the Oceanic and the New York, tied up at pier 38, and as the Titanic eased past them they began to move. The displacement of water and accompanying hydrodynamic forces nearly had damaging results, as suddenly the New York's ropes snapped with several loud reports and she began to be drawn towards the cruising liner like metal to a magnet. Lawrence Beesley heard the ropes break and saw them snaking off into the retreating crowd and the New York coming towards them. The tense scene drew passengers to the rails all along the ship and nearby, one passenger followed the events with a cine camera. Smith and Bowyer, perhaps half expecting this after the Hawke incident, were quick to react. The order was given for 'Full astern' and the starboard anchor was half lowered in case it was necessary to use it quickly. But it was never needed as the prompt actions of the tug Vulcan, which managed to get a line onto the New York, soon averted any danger. The tug took the strain just in time and there were gasps from the crowd as the New York stopped, just eight feet away from the Titanic.

Watching the near accident from first class were millionaire Isidor Straus, his wife Ida and a friend of theirs, Colonel Archibald Gracie, an amateur military historian. As the accident was averted, all of them breathed a sigh of relief. Mr. Straus then noted to Gracie that a few years before, he had taken a trip on the New York, when she had been considered the last word in shipbuilding.

The New York was still adrift and floated clumsily down the River Test held only by the Vulcan, until extra lines were made fast on her. The Oceanic too had strained at her moorings as water first increased then decreased beneath her, but extra ropes had quickly been secured, making her escape impossible. To those of a superstitious nature it seemed an ill omen. However, superstition was not allowed to stop the voyage and once the New York was suitably secured, the Titanic was given permission to proceed.

Having passed beyond the intricate passages of Southampton Water, Pilot Bowyer was dropped off and the Titanic steamed towards the English Channel, past Spithead and the Isle of Wight, which was 'looking superbly beautiful', according to Beesley. They passed a White Star tug, which the ship saluted, and a well-known local photographer on shore, whom Smith acknowledged with a toot of the whistles. Then they were out into a beautiful, glittering sea and the only other ships around seemed to be a cluster of sleek grey warships resting at anchor some distance away. As the Titanic finally left the shores of Britain, a French tricolour was run up her foremast ready for her Channel crossing to Cherbourg.

There were two ports of call before the Titanic set out across the Atlantic Ocean. Cherbourg in France was the first stop and there passengers and mail were taken on board. Many of the new passengers, over 200 in all, were of various European nationalities and some even came from as far afield as the Middle East. However, all were surprised by the size of the ship that was to take them to America.

From Cherbourg, steaming along the Channel after a restful and uneventful night, the Titanic arrived in Queenstown (now named Cobh) in Ireland. There, a similar procedure was gone through, though fewer passengers disembarked or embarked. A small tender chugged out to the liner which stood off at anchor in Queenstown Bay and the exchange of mail and passengers took place.

During this stop, several passengers were surprised to see a head sticking out of the top of the fourth funnel, the ventilation dummy at the back of the ship. A stoker had apparently taken advantage of the lull in activity to climb up from the engine rooms deep below to get a lungful of fresh Irish air. Some of the watchers were alarmed and a few took this as another ill omen. Meanwhile, another stoker, a 24-year old Queenstown man named John Coffey, was smuggling himself aboard the tender. He had not been suffering from premonitions of doom – it seems that he had merely signed aboard the Titanic as a way of earning a free passage home. As the passengers boarded the tender that would take them ashore, Coffey hid himself under some mailbags. Among the passengers leaving the Titanic, meanwhile, was one Father Francis Browne, who had boarded her in Southampton. A keen amateur photographer, Father Browne had spent his couple of days aboard the ship profitably – snapping photos. He took his last couple as he departed the Titanic. One of these was taken from the tender looking up at the starboard wing of the bridge, just in time to capture Captain Smith looking down. It was the last photo ever taken of him.

Coming aboard the ship in the meantime were 113 Irish emigrants off to the United States to start new lives and to seek their fortunes. One of these, Eugene Daly, left his homeland armed with a set of Irish bagpipes and as the tender finally departed from the ship as she prepared for sea, the sound of Daly's pipes playing "Erin's Lament" followed the tender across the water.

At about 1.30 p.m., on 11th April 1912, Smith gave the order for the anchors to be raised and three loud but dreary hoots from the Titanic's whistles joined in the dirge from Daly's pipes. The propellers span, churning up mud and water, and turning a quarter-circle, the Titanic eased herself out of Queenstown Bay. Followed by hundreds of screaming, swooping gulls that danced in the ship's wake until nightfall, the Titanic then set off around the Irish coast towards the open sea and the final long leg of her maiden voyage.

During their first two days aboard the Titanic, the passengers grew familiar with her layout and the daily routine that kept her running. The necessity for routine extended throughout the crew, from the lowliest stoker and ordinary seaman up to Smith himself, who seems to have worked his ship by the book. This meant that every morning, except on Sundays, company rules required a bow to stern, top to bottom inspection of the ship. Each day, at a little after 10 a.m., Smith received in his quarters the chief engineer, purser, assistant purser, surgeon and chief steward, each of whom reported in turn the state of his department. After these reports, at about 10.30, the captain led an entourage of officers through the length and breadth of the ship, from public rooms, dining saloons, bars and corridors to galleys, storerooms and the hospital. While he strode on ahead, the officers behind him took note of his comments on cleanliness and order as he passed through the ship, ready to ensure that any problems were rectified before the next inspection. After the inspection, they all returned to the bridge, where, after the main items of note were out of the way, Smith was left with his command staff as the heads of department returned to their duties. With his staff, the captain discussed the results of his inspection, before taking them all through the day's course for navigation.

At noon each day the officers all gathered on the bridge with their sextants, to take bearings and calculate the ship's position. The general reading was to provide as good an estimate as possible, hopefully ruling out the chance of individual error. Smith noted the result, perhaps checked it himself, and then the estimate was pinned up in the chart room for the purposes of navigation. For the rest of the day the officers went about their usual duties in pre-established shifts. Smith himself was usually found on the bridge, or in his cabin by the wheelhouse, where messages came to him from the bridge or from the wireless room. Long-range messages affecting navigation were received by the wireless operators and on the Titanic the most notable were those concerning the movement of ice fields in the vicinity of the Grand Banks sea lanes, but these were expected, as it was April, and April always brought the icebergs down from the pole.

For the first few days of the journey, the passengers saw little of Smith. When leaving or entering port and of course during bad weather, he always preferred to take his meals on the bridge or in his quarters where he was served by his personal steward, Mr. J.A. Painton. This was the case on the Titanic and for the first day and a half he did not eat in the first-class à la carte restaurant. When he did put in an appearance there, after the ship had departed from Queenstown, he was present during the evening meals, where, contrary to popular belief, he did not sit at a large table surrounded by the finest people, but preferred an ordinary table for six in the dining saloon's centre section. His first appearance there seems to have been on the evening of Friday 12th April and his attendance after that was generally assured. Most of the passengers who met him considered him to be a most charming host, who seemed ever attentive to their needs and to their safety.

Smith was pleased with the way the new liner was behaving, so he obviously felt that he had ample time to accommodate his passengers. Indeed there was only one problem causing him a little anxiety, which was a smouldering fire in a heap of coal down in the boiler section, but Chief Engineer Bell assured him that this was well under control. The fire was finally extinguished on the Sunday morning, saving Smith the rather embarrassing prospect of having to call in the New York fire brigade when they reached the States. But such anxieties and duties aside, the fine weather accompanying the journey found the grand-looking old sea captain strolling the decks and chatting with the passengers, or encountering the odd child wandering through the miles of corridors. One of these was seven-year old Eva Hart, who was accompanied by a large teddy bear, and after asking her where she had got such a large bear and having been told that her father had bought it for her, Smith displayed his easy attitude with children by measuring the little girl against her bear and found the latter to be marginally taller!

The passengers took things easy; many agreed that it was very easy to do so on such a ship. In first class, even Colonel Archibald Gracie, an inveterate fitness fanatic, gave up his usual shipboard routine of rigorous exercise, for the first few days aboard, and succumbed to the luxury that surrounded him, either sitting around reading books borrowed from the ship's library or socialising. In second class, Lawrence Beesley took more notice of what was going on around him. After leaving Queenstown, he spent the afternoon writing letters in the library and he passed a good many of the evenings there, like Gracie, either reading or socialising. But when the mood took him, Beesley wandered the ship, taking in the spectacle and enjoying the sensations of being at sea. He noted that outside the weather was fine and calm, which was reflected in the fact that few people were ever absent from meals. Each morning the sun rose behind them into a sky streaked with clouds that ascended in tiers from red to pink and pink to white as the sun got higher. From second class he could look down over the poop deck and watch the ship's wake, snaking off into infinity behind them. At night, the sun sank before them, 'making an undulating, glittering pathway', for the ship to steam along.

The third-class passengers were enjoying every moment afforded by the fine weather and the novelty of being aboard a ship. The aft well deck provided them with a games field, where impromptu football matches and an uproarious skipping game involving mixed doubles took place. From his overview of the stern, Beesley got used to seeing a few of those in third class. There was one man who often stood alone on the poop deck, who kept himself aloof from the roistering of the "playing field"; Beesley thought that perhaps he was a cultured man who had fallen on hard times. Then there was a man in third class who had managed to afford a second-class ticket for his wife and during the day he used to go and talk to her over the low gate which separated second class from steerage.

Saturday 13th April arrived and with it came increased ice warnings from the Grand Banks area. The President Lincoln, Avala, East Point and Saint Laurent were some of the ships sending out warnings and all of their reports were consistent: 'Field ice, some growlers, some bergs' along the latitude 41° 50'N. However, Saturday passed without incident.

Sunday 14th April dawned. Unlike on the other six days of the week there was no morning inspection; instead there should have been a boat drill but this never happened and it seems that Smith had forsaken the practice and had relied upon a test lowering of a couple of boats before the ship left Southampton. This exercise had taken place under the supervision of Captain Clarke from the Board of Trade. Clarke admitted later on that the practice was a common one and that he had always felt it to be inadequate, but it had become customary and no doubt expedient as it saved time. However, it was always the same members of the crew who carried out these tests, a factor which not only left the greater majority unpractised in lifeboat procedures, but, as events were to prove, not even sure of where their lifeboat stations were.

Because there was no boat drill, Smith appears to have spent most of his early morning on the bridge or in his quarters. Certainly he was on the bridge at 9 a.m., when he received the first of several ice warnings he was to see that day. The wireless message was from the S.S. Caronia:

'Captain, "Titanic" – Westbound steamers report bergs, growlers and field ice in 42°N from 49° to 51°W, 12th April. Compliments – Barr.'

Smith acknowledged receipt of Captain Barr's message.

At 10.30 a.m., Smith made his way to the first-class dining saloon, where divine service was held. This was attended by a good many of the passengers and Smith led them in prayers drawn from the White Star Line's own prayer book. Among the congregation was Colonel Gracie, who, disgusted at his lethargy over the last few days, had been up early before breakfast for a vigorous game of squash with the ship's squash professional, F. Wright. Gracie had then had his breakfast before attending divine service. He noticed with interest the large gathering and came away impressed with the "Prayer For Those At Sea".

Two sisters, Martha Stevenson and Elizabeth Eustis, were also there. Near neighbours of the millionaire Thayers in Haverford, Martha and Elizabeth had so far enjoyed the trip and had spent the earlier part of Sunday morning writing letters saying so, before they went to join the congregation in the restaurant. They too enjoyed the service, though they came away surprised that they had not sung "For Those In Peril On The Sea".

In second class, Lawrence Beesley attended a separate service for the passengers there, which was conducted in the saloon by Mr. McElroy, the ship's purser.

The service in first class ended at about 11.15, with the singing of the hymn, "Oh God Our Help In Ages Past". Soon after this, Smith was back on the bridge where at noon, as usual, the officers gathered with their sextants to "shoot the sun" and, in accordance with company rules, the ship's whistles and engine room telegraphs were tested and found to be in working order.

While the passengers enjoyed their dinners, sat reading or took a turn around the sun deck, more ice warnings reached the Titanic. At 1.42 p.m., Jack Phillips, the chief Marconi wireless operator on the Titanic, received a call from the S.S. Baltic:

'Captain Smith, "Titanic" – have had moderate, variable winds and clear, fine weather since leaving. Greek steamer "Athenai" reports passing icebergs and large quantities of field ice today in lat.41°51' N, long. 49°52' W. Last night we spoke German oiltank steamer "Deutschland", Stettin to Philadelphia, not under control, short of coal, lat. 40°42' N, long. 55°11'W. Wishes to be reported to New York and other steamers. Wish you and "Titanic" all success – Commander.'

Smith received this message as he stood talking to J. Bruce Ismay. After scanning its contents, he handed the note over to Ismay who, after reading it, put the paper in his pocket. This should have gone straight to the navigation room, but instead, Ismay later showed the note to some of the passengers. It was 7.15 p.m. before Smith remembered the note and asked for it to be returned and only then was it posted in the chart room.

At 1.45 p.m., a message was relayed to the Titanic from the German steamer Amerika: '"Amerika" passed two large icebergs in 41°27' N, 50°8' W, on the 14th April.' Perhaps because this message was not directly addressed to the captain, Phillips does not seem to have thought of sending it up to the bridge and none of the officers there ever recalled having seen this message. Ironically, it placed bergs and an ice field immediately south of the impending point of collision.

Contrary to later accusations that Smith had blatantly ignored these ice warnings, Ismay, still walking around with the earlier message in his pocket, concluded from his chat with Smith that they would be up into ice 'that night'. The indications were that it had been a mild winter on the pole and that all sorts of icy debris were coming down with the Labrador Current, to areas much further south than was usually known. Smith seems to have made some effort to counter this, because at 5.50 p.m., as a number of officers noticed, his navigation orders called for a course alteration to a more southerly route than that normally taken by transatlantic liners. The situation is perhaps best explained in the official report of the British inquiry under Lord Mersey:

'At 5.50 p.m., the "Titanic's" course (which had been S 62°W) was changed to bring her on a westerly course for New York. In ordinary circumstances this change in her course should have been made half an hour earlier, but she seems on this occasion to have continued for about ten minutes longer on her south-westerly course before turning, with the result that she found herself, after altering course at 5.50 p.m., about four or five miles south of the customary route and four miles south and considerably to the westward of the indicated position of the "Baltic's" ice.'

Even so, the inquiry still had its reservations: 'This change of course was so insignificant that in my opinion it cannot have been made in consequence of information as to ice.'

However, there seems to have been no other reason for it. But if he had made this 'insignificant' course alteration on account of ice reports, Smith does not seem to have felt that the situation warranted a decrease in the ship's speed. The engines were still whirring away at 75 revolutions, pushing the Titanic along at approximately $21\frac{1}{2}$ knots. This was a fact touched upon more than once at the subsequent inquiries.

The passengers lounged, unaware of the dangers ahead. Martha Stevenson and Elizabeth Eustis had, after finishing their reading, taken tea outside, which they rounded off with a walk around the boat deck. It was during this afternoon, though, that they, like many others, began to notice how very much colder the weather was than before.

In second class, Lawrence Beesley sheltered from the cold in the library, where he spent the afternoon chatting to a shipboard acquaintance, the Reverend Carter of the Church of England, who was making the crossing with his wife. They discussed the relative merits of their old universities, as Reverend Carter had been to Oxford, while Beesley was a former Cambridge student. The conversation then moved onto parish matters before the reverend hunted out the purser for permission to use the saloon for an evening prayer meeting, and this was granted.

Beesley remembered well that last afternoon on the Titanic and the lounges with their armchairs and small tables dotted around, the polished mahogany fittings and the clean, white fluted columns. Through the windows was a covered corridor 'reserved by general consent as a children's playground' where two young boys played with their doting father, Michael Navratil, who called himself "Mr. Hoffman" and had kidnapped his sons from his wife in an attempt to save his troubled marriage! Nearby was a man in a grey knickerbocker suit. He too had a couple of children, one of whom he usually carried. Over his shoulder was slung a camera.

Also there were two American ladies, dressed all in white, one of whom was returning home from India via England. Both chatted with a very distinguished-looking gentleman, who was a recent acquaintance of theirs. They were deep in their talk, but this stopped when they were interrupted by a child who wanted them to pay attention to a large doll she was carrying in her arms.

In a far corner sat a young couple and Beesley recognised the cinematographer who had filmed the near collision with the New York. The man's young French wife sat beside him playing patience while he looked on.

Two Catholic priests sat reading in the middle of the library. Near to them was a young fire engineer on his way to Mexico.

Then there were the smiling lift boys in their mid-teens, one of whom had said wistfully to Beesley that he wished he could go outside once in a while.

Beesley later recalled with sadness that he never encountered any of these people aboard the ship that later rescued the survivors from the Titanic.

Not long after this, the passengers sat down for what for most was their last meal. In first class, George Graham, who had recently been in the Potteries as a buyer for a Winnipeg company, was seated for his meal with two fellow buyers: Spencer V. Silverthorne of St. Louis, a buyer for Nugent's department store, and James R. McGough, a buyer for Gimbels of Philadelphia. Edward P. Calderhead of New York and J.I. Flynn were also seated with them and were probably in the same trade. They perhaps talked shop as they tucked into meals drawn from a menu that offered: Consommé Olga, Cream of Barley, Sauté of Chicken, Lamb in Mint Sauce, Duck in Apple Sauce, Sirloin of Beef, Chateau Potatoes and assorted vegetables, followed by Waldorf Pudding, Peaches in Chartreuse Jelly, Chocolate and Vanilla Eclairs and French Ice Cream. As a memento of the meal, they reserved one of the souvenir menus and each in turn scribbled his name and address on the back.

In second class, an equally sumptuous meal was served, though one that was a bit too rich for some palates, like that of Charlotte Collyer who, not long after the meal, retired to her cabin to suffer in silence.

At 6 p.m., Second Officer Lightoller took over from Chief Officer Wilde on the bridge watch. Smith was not present at the time. He was probably in his cabin preparing to visit the first-class dining saloon as he had been invited to spend a few hours that evening at a private party hosted by the Widener family.

At 7.30 p.m., the Titanic's wireless operators intercepted a message from the Leyland Line steamer Californian, to the Antillian. The Californian, ahead of the Titanic on a more northerly route, was to play a controversial part in the night ahead. The message, meantime, was as follows:

'To Captain, "Antillian", 6.30 p.m. apparent ship's time; lat. 42° 3'N, long. 49° 9'W. Three large bergs five miles to southward of us. Regards. – Lord.'

The message was delivered to the bridge by the junior Marconi operator, Harold Bride, but he did not remember to which officer.

The British inquiry found that at the time of the collision, the Titanic had long since passed the danger posed by these bergs, as she was 50 miles to the westward of the reported sighting. The inquiry also felt that the small ice reported earlier by the Caronia would most likely have drifted well to the eastward and the large bergs still in the powerful tow of the Labrador Current would have been taken further south.

Smith does not seem to have been informed about the message from the Californian. By that time, he was no longer in his cabin, but had gone down to the first-class restaurant where he joined the first-class passengers who had been invited to the Wideners' party. Among the invited guests were John and Marian Thayer and their son Jack, Major Archibald Butt and Henry B. Harris, the theatrical director, and his wife. Mrs. Harris had come to the party with an injured arm and Smith, seeing her trouble, went over to her table and congratulated her on her spirit. He then seated himself at his usual table, where he was joined by the Thayers. With them he spent an enjoyable evening and allowed himself to unwind a little; he puffed his way through two of his favourite cigars, but drank nothing alcoholic. After the disaster, one passenger (who had been seated at another table) claimed that she had seen the captain drinking, but this was countered by depositions from Mrs. Thayer and Mrs. Widener, both of whom stated that not once had they seen Smith drinking that night.

Back on the bridge, Herbert Lightoller was still on watch.

Despite the fact that the ship was past the positions outlined in the several ice warnings so far, Lightoller was still well aware that there was ice in the immediate vicinity. He recalled that earlier in the day, at about 12.45 p.m., just before he was to go off watch, Smith had shown him the Caronia message and Lightoller had made a rough calculation in his head that the ship would be up to the ice at about 9.30 p.m. A little later, Lightoller had asked Sixth Officer Moody for his opinion and Moody had said that 11 p.m. would be the approximate time. Though puzzled at the discrepancy, Lightoller presumed that Moody had seen a message which he had not. Nonetheless, the crux of the discussion at least was that they were heading into an ice region and that they would be in it before midnight. This did not worry the second officer; it was a clear, fine, beautiful starlit night, and he believed that he would be able to spot even a growler with 'sufficient distinctness' at a distance of up to two miles.

At about 8.55, as the meal had ended earlier than expected, Smith excused himself from the dinner party and made his way back to the bridge. There he met Lightoller and talked to him about the weather.

'There is not much wind,' said Smith.

'No, it is a flat calm,' replied Lightoller.

Smith echoed the remark. Lightoller then added that it was a pity that the wind would not be following them into the ice region, where its effect would cause ripples around the icebergs making them more visible.

'In any case,' Lightoller continued, 'there will be a certain amount of reflected light from the bergs.'

'Oh yes, there will be a certain amount of reflected light,' said Smith.

Lightoller further noted that even with the blue side of any berg towards them, there would remain a white outline, which, he felt, would still give them sufficient warning. Smith agreed. Lightoller did not, however, discuss with Smith the discrepancy between his own and Moody's calculations as to when they would reach the ice.

The captain remained on the bridge for about 25 minutes until around 9.20 p.m., at which time he decided to retire to his cabin.

'If it becomes at all doubtful,' he said to Lightoller as he turned to go, 'let me know at once. I shall be just inside.' Lightoller understood this to refer to ice.

As soon as Smith left, Lightoller told Sixth Officer Moody to ring up the crow's nest. The lookouts were 'to keep a sharp lookout for ice, particularly small ice and growlers'. Moody did so and told the men to pass the message on when their shift ended. Lightoller himself kept his eyes peeled.

In the Marconi room at about 9.30 p.m., Jack Phillips was busy sending communications via Cape Race shore station, but at one point, though, he cut off to take a message from the steamer, Mesaba:

'From "Mesaba" to "Titanic" and all eastbound ships. Ice report in lat. 42°N to 41° 25'N, long. 49° to long. 50° 30'W. Saw much heavy pack ice and a great number large icebergs. Also field ice. Weather good, clear.'

This message placed ice in the immediate vicinity, but as with the earlier message, it never reached the bridge – had it done so it may have had an effect on the way the ship was navigated.

Lightoller's watch on the bridge ended at 10 p.m. when First Officer Murdoch took over, to give a fresh pair of eyes on the lookout. Lightoller drew Murdoch's attention to the night order book that carried a footnote about possible ice and the message was initialled by each officer in turn. Lightoller said to the first officer, 'We might be up around the ice any time now.' Murdoch, however, was well aware of the situation, as shown by the subsequent testimony of the lamp trimmer, Samuel Hemmings, who had reported to Murdoch at about 7.15 that evening that the lamps were all in order. Murdoch had then said, 'Hemmings, when you go forward see the forescuttle is closed as we are in the vicinity of ice, and there is a glow coming from that, and I want everything dark before the bridge.' Hemmings had done the job.

Murdoch took up his place on the unlit bridge; the only light before him now, but out of sight, was a mast light high above the crow's nest. In the crow's nest at 10 p.m., a similar changeover took place with the lookouts and the first act of the tragedy had gained its opening players.

6

Iceberg Right Ahead

Lookouts Frederick Fleet and Reginald Lee came on duty at 10 p.m. and after climbing up inside the mast, they took over in the crow's nest from the earlier shift, who warned them prophetically to watch out for icebergs. The two men were well wrapped up against the cold air, the temperature of which had by then dropped to 32°F (0°C); however, on the plus side, it was a cloudless night and their field of vision was clear. It emerged at the later inquiries that the lookouts should have been issued with binoculars, but these seem to have been misplaced from the beginning of the voyage. Fred Fleet always insisted afterwards that had they been issued with binoculars – the tools of their trade as he saw them – then the tragedy would have been averted. In the meantime, though, they did not need them, because as well as it being a clear starlit night, the sea was as calm as a lake and as of yet there was no sign of the ice they had been warned to look out for.

The scent of the night air gave Elizabeth Shutes the shivers in her first-class cabin; the air was biting cold and had with it a clamminess that reminded her of an ice cave she had seen on the Eiger glacier. She lay in her cabin, slowly growing more aware of the all-pervading chill until she could stand it no more and stood up to switch on the stove, which soon warmed her room. She liked travelling by ship, she decided, but the cold of the night air made her nervous.

Jack Thayer was still in the ship's public rooms and well insulated from the icy air outside. He had struck up a conversation with another well-to-do young man named Long, the son of a Massachusetts judge. The two of them were in need of company: Mr. Long was travelling alone and Jack's parents were in the restaurant talking to the other guests who were still at the Wideners' party. The two young men lounged around idly in their dinner suits, talking about where they had recently been on holiday in Europe and Jack also touched on his hobby of stamp collecting, which he indulged in during his travels. Their conversation developed into a healthy rapport, so much so, that when the Thayers came downstairs two hours later, the two new friends parted with hopes that they might continue their talk the next day. Long suggested that Jack might join him for a walk on the deck in the morning, then he said goodnight to the Thayers before going for a stroll outside. Jack and his parents returned to their cabins.

In second class after dinner, the Reverend Carter had invited his acquaintances and anyone who was interested to join in the evening service he had arranged to be held in the saloon. When everyone had turned up, there were over a hundred people gathered there. With Carter leading the service and a man being available to play the piano for the hymn-singing, the reverend then asked the congregation to offer suggestions as to what they should sing. Several suitable hymns were chosen, one being "For Those In Peril On The Sea", which Elizabeth Eustis and Martha Stevenson had lamented the lack of earlier that day. According to Lawrence Beesley, the old sailors' hymn was sung in 'hushed tones'.

The singing ended at about 10 p.m., when they saw the stewards standing around waiting to serve up coffee and biscuits before going off duty. Beesley joined the Carters over coffee and chatted for a time before he decided to retire for the night. At 10.45, he returned to his cabin, where he lay on his bunk, quiet and undisturbed. The only noises by then were sounds coming through the ventilators of stewards talking and moving around the corridors; the only sensation was a light, lulling vibration to the bed, caused by the distant hum of the ship's engines.

The Titanic sailed further on into the dark night. In the galleys the bakers put in the loaves for the next day, while the "boots" did his rounds collecting shoes for a new overnight polish and the dining room stewards cleared away after the meals. The stokers, firemen and engineers of the 8 to 12 shift sweated down below in temperatures in the 80°s to 90°s F. In his wireless cabin, Jack Phillips worked alone passing on the large volume of passenger messages to Cape Race. Ships' wireless was still something of a novelty with the passengers and with it being the maiden voyage of the wonderful new Titanic, many thought that it was the perfect occasion on which to send greetings to their family and friends. Phillips felt that he was overworked and he was not in the mood for interruptions.

The Leyland Line steamer, Californian, had by then stopped in field ice. She was still ahead of the Titanic and about 10 to 19 miles to the north; her captain, Stanley Lord, had ordered extra ice warnings to ships in the area. The Californian's wireless operator, Cyril Evans, dutifully called up the Titanic, but as the ships were so close to each other, the boosted signal when it came through his headphones nearly deafened Jack Phillips, who in turn cut in on Evans with a terse transmission of his own: 'Keep out! Shut up! You're jamming my signal. I'm working Cape Race.'

The Californian's operator had no option but to shut up, though out of interest he listened in to the new liner's wireless traffic for about another half an hour. Evans had been up early that morning and had stayed on duty longer than usual. He was tired and when he finally gave up listening to the Titanic it was 11.30 p.m., so he switched off his set and went to bed. The Californian was only a small steamer and carried but one wireless operator, who was soon fast asleep, so there was no-one listening a short time later when the Titanic began sending messages of a far different nature.

In the Titanic's crow's nest at about this time, lookout Reg Lee thought that a slight haze had begun to form in the air, though Fred Fleet said he never noticed it. If a haze had been forming though, it may go some way to explaining why neither man reported seeing the telltale "ice blink", where ice on the horizon reflects the starlight and which, with an ice field, gives the effect of a shimmering white line in the distance. Seven bells struck at 11.30 and the minutes, 11.31 ... 32 ... 33 ticked by. At 11.40 p.m., Fleet was looking forward into the darkness ahead when something caught his eye. There was a darker patch there and when suddenly a large indistinct shape loomed out of the darkness, Fleet realised with a jolt what it was. 60 feet out of the water and 500 yards dead ahead was an iceberg. Eyewitnesses later either described it or drew it as triple-peaked and tapering down to the sea. Newspapers making use of dramatic hyperbole referred to it as 'a monstrous berg' and 'a mountain of ice', though by iceberg standards it was unremarkable – at its highest it was only level with the Titanic's boat deck, but it was still dangerous! Without a word to Lee, Fleet turned and rang the alarm bell three times, which signified 'Object ahead', then he reached across Lee and grabbed the telephone to the bridge, which was answered by Sixth Officer Moody.

'Are you there?' asked Fleet.

'Yes. What do you see?'

'Iceberg right ahead.'

Moody paused before saying, 'Thank you' and quickly relayed the message to First Officer Murdoch, who glanced ahead before calling out instinctively, 'Hard-a-starboard' to the helmsman, which, under the helm orders then in use, turned the ship to port. Murdoch then ordered the engine room to 'Stop engines and full astern' and he pulled the lever which closed the watertight doors below sea level.

Incredibly, despite the constant ice warnings, before Murdoch ordered the engines to stop, the Titanic was still travelling at a breakneck 21½ knots and even when the liner's three mighty screws were thrown into full astern, the ship still careered forward at a high speed. The helmsman turned the wheel as far as it would go and after several seconds, the ship's nose began to swing to port.

In the crow's nest, Fleet and Lee gripped the railings, watching tensely as the berg came towards them, suddenly glittering into life as the ship's lights flared across its surface as she swept past. The lookouts noted that one of the peaks glowed with an almost phosphorescent glare. Fleet and Lee held their breaths, but gasped with relief when the berg passed to starboard and nothing seemed to happen. It had been a close shave.

It was too close, for as the ship gently brushed the berg, an action which scattered chunks of ice along the boat deck, a light shudder passed through the ship which could be felt by the crew on the bridge, but not by Fleet and Lee.

Many of the passengers never noticed the collision, but those who did said that it seemed as if the ship had passed over a thousand marbles and that there had been an ominous sound, like tearing calico, that had accompanied the quivering sensation. Lawrence Beesley thought that the ship gave a momentary heave and that there was a brief change to the vibrating pattern of the engines which he could feel through his bunk. This did not alarm him and when he did eventually grow curious enough to leave his cabin, it was to see why the ship had stopped.

In her first-class stateroom, Marian Thayer, who had dined at the captain's table earlier that evening, had just called for her steward to open a porthole; the man was halfway across the room when there was a slight but prolonged jarring sensation that passed through the ship. Her actions and those of her family were more immediate than Beesley's, and throwing on their coats, they went up onto A deck to see what had happened.

Elizabeth Shutes felt the quiver run underneath her as she lay on her bed and she jumped up in surprise, but, trusting to the safe reputation of the vessel, she lay back down. Moments later, though, there was a knock at her door and she heard the voice of her friend, Mrs. Graham, saying, 'Come quickly to my cabin; an iceberg has just passed our window; I know we have just struck one.'

In the third-class accommodation for single male passengers, Norwegian emigrant, Olaus Abelseth, awoke with a start.

'What is that?' asked his room mate.

'I don't know,' Abelseth replied, 'but we had better get up.'

Back in first class, Margaret "Molly" Brown, an irrepressible Denver socialite, had been reading in her room until there was an almighty crash at her window that threw her to the floor. When she got up to see what they had hit there was nothing to be seen, so she settled back down to her book.

Hugh Woolner, another first-class passenger, had installed himself and a group of friends in the smoking room on A deck. A sumptuous male sanctuary, the smoking room was the place the men traditionally retired to after a meal, there to sit and smoke in luxury, bury themselves in books or drink and gamble. Woolner and his friends were involved in a light-hearted game of bridge, when they experienced the bumping, grinding jolt of the impact that seemed to start far off in the bow and run the length of the ship, rattling her beneath their feet. Woolner jumped up, and he and a companion rushed outside via the swinging doors onto the promenade deck. Unaccustomed to the dark they could see little, but nearby, somebody was calling out that they had struck an iceberg.

As the shudder of the collision died away, Captain Smith rushed onto the bridge from his cabin beside the wheelhouse.

'Mr. Murdoch, what was that?' he asked.

'An iceberg, sir. I hard-a-starboarded and reversed the engines, and I was going to hard-a-port around it, but she was too close. I couldn't do any more.'

'Close the emergency doors.'

'The doors are already closed.'

Smith immediately went to the starboard wing of the bridge and stuck his head out of the window. Murdoch and Fourth Officer Boxhall trailed along behind him. Boxhall thought that he could see a dark shape far astern.

Second Officer Lightoller had, after finishing his watch, done his rounds, then gone to bed. Now, woken by the collision, he went out onto the deck in his bare feet. Looking forward he caught sight of Smith and Murdoch peering out of the window, but he could make out nothing more and there seemed to be no obvious damage to the ship.

Dr. Washington Dodge in first class thought likewise. Like several others he had rushed outside to see what the ship had struck, but there was nothing visible by then, just a few low ridges of ice bobbing around them. He decided to return to his cabin, as there seemed to be no danger, and he had just turned to go when he bumped into a couple of stokers who had suddenly appeared unannounced on the promenade deck.

'Do you think there is any danger, sir?' one of them asked Dodge.

'If there is any danger it would be due to the vessel's having sprung a leak, and you ought to know more about that than I.'

The stokers suddenly appeared startled and replied with alarm:

'Well, sir, the water was pouring into the stoke'old when we came up, sir.'

Those in the stokeholds, boiler rooms and engine rooms already knew the worst of it, that water was gushing into the first five of the ship's watertight compartments. In the past it was thought by many that the iceberg had gouged a 300-feet long gash along the Titanic; the writer Joseph Conrad described the Titanic as having been ripped open 'like a Huntley and Palmer biscuit box'. But the findings of Dr. Robert Ballard and the team that located the wreck of the Titanic in 1985 seemed to confirm what a few researchers had already guessed. Under the force of the impact it appears rather that the ship's plates had buckled inwards on a spur of ice, rivets had been popped and gaps had been opened between the sheets of metal forming the hull. Rather than a continuous gash, there were intermittent holes in the hull where the plates of steel had parted. The line of rupture came above the double-bottomed hull, where the iceberg bump-bump-bumping along the ship had punched holes in her about fifteen feet above the keel, through which powerful jets of water then blasted. Within the first ten minutes of the impact, the rate of increase of the water put its level fourteen feet above the keel in the forepeak, with comparable levels in all of the first five compartments.

The leading fireman, Fred Barratt, in boiler room no. 6 (in compartment no. 5), had been chatting to Second Engineer Hesketh when the boiler room indicator suddenly flashed to the "STOP" position. No sooner had Hesketh called out the order 'Shut all dampers', so cutting the air supply to the boiler furnaces, than alarm bells started ringing and the red lights flashed above the emergency doors as, on the bridge, Murdoch threw the switch to close them. The engineers and staff had only a few seconds to wonder what was happening, as suddenly there was a loud bang, 'like a big gun going off,' and somebody shouted a warning. The starboard wall must have rippled as the finger of the iceberg ran along it, then the ship's skin cracked and Hesketh and Barratt were hit by a jet of ice-cold water that so shocked them that they dashed through the closing emergency door, leaving the remaining men to quickly draw the fires in the boilers as the water flowed first around the pipes and then up around their knees. Once this job was done, the men escaped up the ladders to the comparative safety of E deck.

On the other side of the emergency door, Hesketh and Barratt found the scene in boiler room no. 5 to be just as confused, as the plates there had also given slightly beyond the watertight bulkhead. Confusion reigned in the "blackgang"; men were digging themselves out of mounds of fallen coal, officers were shouting and no-one was sure of what had happened, though someone guessed that they had run aground off Newfoundland. Not all the engineering staff were on duty at the time, but the sounding of a warning bell whilst at sea and at such a time of night was instantly recognised as an emergency call and in a few minutes everyone was downstairs.

On the bridge, Smith turned away from the window and ordered Boxhall to go and check the forward area. As Boxhall left, the captain wandered back into the wheelhouse and laid his hands on the engine room telegraph which he moved to "Half Ahead". He then sent the stand-by quartermaster to Chief Engineer Bell for a damage report. By the time the man came back, the engines had stopped for good.

Boxhall returned and reported that he had been as far forward as steerage accommodation allowed and that there was no damage, but Smith was not so sure.

'Go down and find the carpenter and get him to sound the ship,' he said.

Boxhall again went on his way, but he had only reached the stairs when the flustered carpenter appeared, gasping, 'She's making water fast, sir.'

There followed one of the mail clerks from the post office in the forecastle, with news that the mail room was flooding. He and his four companions had already started their devoted, but ultimately pointless, attempt to drag all the mailbags to the higher decks. Boxhall checked this, then several minutes later came back with bad news, which was all that Smith needed to know. The ship was breached heavily below the water line, the water was by then 24 feet above the keel in the forepeak and the heavy mailbags in the post office were floating. Compartments 1 to 5 were filling up rapidly and boiler room no. 5 in the 6th compartment had also started to flood, but pumps were being brought into action there and seemed to be keeping the water level down. Nearby, the ship's commutator, a device that showed the angle of the ship's bow, registered an unhealthy list to the liner's nose. Smith cast a glance at it and muttered 'My God!', then composed himself as Thomas Andrews, the Harland and Wolff managing director, appeared.

Andrews, a brilliant engineer and ship designer, knew more about the Titanic –its construction, its capabilities, its strengths and its weaknesses –than anyone else on board. Dedicated to the perfection of his work, he had spent the last few days assessing the ship's performance and checking for any aspects of her design that were in need of alteration. To this end he had spent most of that Sunday evening in his cabin, A36, studying the Titanic's plans; he had been so absorbed in his work that, like many, he appears not to have noticed the collision and knew nothing of the ship's predicament, until there was a knock at his door and a messenger sent by the captain asked him if he could come to the bridge urgently. When he got there, Smith informed Andrews of what had happened and asked him if he would accompany him on an inspection of the ship. The two men went forward, keeping to the crew's companionways rather than the usual corridors, so as to avoid alarming the passengers. Viewing the damage with a critical eye, Andrews took note of the water levels and their rate of increase. After ten minutes they returned to the bridge and conferred briefly before Smith posed the question uppermost in his mind: 'How long have we?'

Both of them realised by then that the damage done to the ship was enough to sink her. With the first five compartments gone, it was as if by divine intervention that the iceberg had inflicted just enough damage to show up the Titanic's single weakness in her seemingly impregnable system of bulkheads. In the bow, the bulkheads separating the first five compartments were of equal height and reached up to at least E deck. However, the bulkhead separating compartments 5 and 6 was smaller than those before it. With three of its compartments flooded, the Titanic would have limped into New York; with four flooded, the ship would still have floated, but with the first five flooded, compartment no. 5 would spill over into compartment no. 6, then into nos. 7, 8, 9 and so on –

this was a mathematical certainty. What was not certain was the amount of time they had left. Andrews found a scrap of paper and quickly jotted down a series of figures before saying, 'An hour and a half. Possibly two. Not much longer.'

With this final confirmation of his worst fears, Smith did not hesitate and snapped a swift order to Chief Officer Wilde to uncover the boats. It was then 12.05 a.m. on Monday 15th April and Smith instructed his other officers as they came to him. First Officer Murdoch was ordered to rouse the passengers, Mr. Moody to find out the list for the lifeboat stations and Boxhall was told to go and wake up Second Officer Lightoller and Third Officer Pitman. Chief Engineer Bell also briefly appeared and Smith received assurances that Bell and his men would do their best to keep a power supply running to the pumps and the ship's lights. When Boxhall reappeared, Smith sent him to the chart room to work out their position and the fourth officer promptly vanished through the door and got to work. Smith turned back to Mr. Andrews and was talking to him quietly when J. Bruce Ismay appeared on the bridge, with his pyjamas tucked under his suit. Ismay wanted to know why the ship had stopped and Smith informed him about the iceberg.

'Do you think the ship is seriously damaged?' asked Ismay. The old captain looked grim and replied, 'I'm afraid she is.'

The Marconi wireless operator, Harold Bride, later recalled the first time he heard about the collision. He was standing by Phillips, ready to take over the shift from the senior operator, when Smith stuck his head into the cabin and said:

'We've struck an iceberg and I'm having an inspection made to tell us what it has done for us. You'd better get ready to send out a call for assistance. But don't send it until I tell you.'

Ten minutes later, at about 12.15 a.m., the captain returned. There was by then a great deal of noise outside, but to Bride's mind this did not indicate trouble. This time Smith barely put his head through the door.

'Send the call for assistance,' he said, and handed over Boxhall's hastily scribbled estimate of their position, which was 41°, 46′N, 50°, 14′W.

'What call should I send?' asked Phillips.

'The regulation international call for help. Just that,' the captain replied and left.

Outside, Second Officer Lightoller met Smith, 'his face stern but haggard', just as he was leaving the wireless room. Several minutes earlier, the boilers had been closed down and with a tremendous roar, the steam was being vented from them via the boiler relief pipes against the funnels. The noise was deafening. Lightoller, who had been helping to uncover the boats, had been looking around for Smith. Having found him, he had to cup his hands to the captain's ear and shout to ask him whether the boats should be swung out. Smith nodded and added that they should start getting the passengers to their boat stations. Lightoller left him and passed the order along that the boats were to be swung out ready for loading. Lightoller had earlier asked Chief Officer Wilde if the boats should be swung out and Wilde had said not, so Lightoller had gone over his head. Several minutes later, when the boats were out, he again went to Wilde, this time for the word to start filling the boats. However, the order was 'No' again, so Lightoller once more sought out Smith, whom he found on the bridge. Smith listened to Lightoller before nodding and urging him on, saying, according to some sources, 'Yes, put the women and children in and lower away.'

The passengers had by this time begun to notice that something was amiss. Marian Thayer had been walking around the ship, trying to account for the jolt that had got her out of her room, and it was not long before she saw that the ship was dipping to the bow and starboard. Lawrence Beesley noticed a strange effect when he tried the stairs. The steps seemed level, but when he put his feet down on them he found that his centre of gravity had shifted and his feet didn't land where they should have done; it was as if the ship were down at the bow.

One crew member in his bunk was woken by the sound of air whistling out of a forward locker as it was forced out of the forepeak tank by the rising sea water. One third-class passenger, emigrant Daniel Buckley, had slept through the collision, but had woken up a few moments later, as he must have sensed that something was wrong. When he got up he, 'jumped out on the floor' and found that he was standing in a spreading pool of sea water:

'The water was just coming in silently. I told the other fellows to get up, that there was something wrong and that the water was coming in. They only laughed at me. One of them says, "Get back into bed. You're not in Ireland now." I got on my clothes as quick as I could, and the three other fellows got out. The room was very small, so I got out to give them room to dress themselves. Two sailors came along and they were shouting, "All up on the deck unless you want to get drowned!" '

The five dedicated postal clerks in the forward post office had to give up their attempts to save the mail, as they found themselves rapidly shoved out of the mail room as the rising sea water left it in disarray. They were forced up a stairwell, from where they looked down at the flood below them. There they were joined for a short time by a couple of passengers, then by Boxhall and briefly by Smith himself, probably when he and Andrews were inspecting the damage.

Back in first class, the passengers wanted to know what was happening, but as yet, no-one was getting any answers. Elizabeth Shutes had joined her friend Mrs. Graham and her daughter Margaret in their cabin. Presently, a stewardess appeared, but she could tell them nothing, so Elizabeth looked into the corridor and saw people appearing from behind half-closed doors to ask questions. Everyone was puzzled and a little ill at ease, but there was still no excitement. Elizabeth sat down and began talking to Mrs. Graham's daughter. Margaret was trying to appear calm and was munching on a chicken sandwich, but her hand shook so badly that the chicken kept falling out from the bread and her fear was so apparent that for the first time Elizabeth herself felt a wave of nervousness overtaking her. A few moments later an officer passed the cabin door and she sought reassurance.

'Is there an accident or danger of any kind?' Elizabeth asked.

'None so far as I know,' the officer replied quietly and kindly. But Elizabeth was not so sure and when the same officer entered a nearby cabin she listened and heard him say, 'We can keep the water out for a while.'

Back in the wireless cabin, Phillips had begun to tap out "CQD", the old form of distress signal; "CQ" meant 'Attention all stations' and "D" indicated that it was a distress call. This was followed by the letters "MGY", the Titanic's registration. However, at this time there was little in the way of distress in the two operators, who actually found their situation rather comical and for five minutes or so they were cracking jokes with one another. They, like most of the passengers, must have felt at this point that their actions were rather over-cautious – after all, surely the Titanic was unsinkable? Nonetheless, Phillips transmitted the signal for assistance and after several other vessels had heard it, he contacted the Olympic, the Titanic's sister ship. She was 500 miles away and it was as they were taking her call that Smith reappeared and asked,

'What are you sending?'

'CQD,' replied Phillips.

Bride was on form and cracked a remark that brought a laugh even from his increasingly worried captain:

'Send SOS. It's the new call and it may be your last chance to send it!'

The black humour of the remark struck Phillips as being particularly funny and so, switching the signal, he broadcast one of the world's first SOS distress calls.

All across the Atlantic shipping lanes, vessels were picking up the Titanic's cry for help: the Olympic (500 miles away), Mount Temple (49 miles), Frankfort (153 miles), Birma (70 miles), Baltic (243 miles), Virginian (170 miles) and many more. On a more southerly route, the Cunard liner Carpathia was 58 miles away on the right side of the ice field. Her wireless man, Harold Cottam, was on the bridge when the first CQD was sounded. Shortly afterwards, he returned to his radio cabin and decided to put in a courtesy call to the new White Star liner, which he knew to be nearby. It came as a total surprise, therefore, when Cottam heard Phillips reply that the Titanic had struck a berg and needed help badly. That he could scarcely credit what he was hearing was evident in the way Cottam had to ask Phillips for advice – should he tell his captain? Phillips replied, 'Yes, quick.'

The Carpathia's skipper was Captain Arthur Rostron, a man whose most notable moment up to this point in time was that he had once claimed to have seen a sea monster. Though some may have scoffed, this nonetheless marked out Rostron as a man of some imagination, which in this instance was to serve him well. Once he had received the news from the excited wireless operator, Rostron paused only long enough to ask Cottam if he was sure that it was the Titanic. When Cottam replied in the affirmative, Rostron dressed and began giving orders. Had she been a military ship, it would have been appropriate to say that the Carpathia's decks were cleared for action. The ship was immediately turned to the ailing liner's reported position. Rostron called on his engineers for everything they could give him and he got it. The ship's top speed of $14^1/_2$ knots rose to an amazing $17^1/_2$ knots which made the bulkheads shudder and gave the engineers nightmares about a possible boiler explosion. Ladders were fixed over the side, oil was made ready to be pumped around the ship to keep the water calm, the passengers were asked to keep to their bunks and space was set aside for survivors. Extra blankets were taken out, the ship's three doctors were told to expect patients and extra lookouts were posted on the bow and on the bridge. Rostron made it very clear that they would be entering an ice region and that he expected everyone to be on their toes. Cottam, meanwhile, returned to his wireless and assured Phillips that they were 'coming hard'.

The Carpathia was four hours distant even at her breakneck speed. Yet, from the bridge of the Titanic could be seen a tantalising light to the north – a ship on the horizon which was seemingly so near, yet so far because Phillips was unable to raise her. The subsequent inquiries in both America and Britain deemed this ship to be the Leyland steamer, Californian, whose wireless operator had earlier been brushed aside by the irritable Phillips. After the disaster, her captain, Stanley Lord, was censured by both inquiries, since her officers had observed rockets and the lights of a vessel off to the south. Lord had taken ample precautions with his own ship, more so than Smith, but during the critical hours that night he had been asleep below and perhaps only half heard or understood the reports from his officers of a ship firing rockets, which he took to be company signals of some sort. Evidence for and against the Californian being the ship seen from the Titanic is extant and Lord was later to find himself cast in the role of the scapegoat in a controversy that has lasted to this day.

Fourth Officer Boxhall was one of those who noticed the lights of a ship to the north and at some time after midnight he reported it to Smith. To Boxhall, the light seemed only about five miles away and the junior officer suggested firing distress rockets, to which Smith agreed. Quartermaster George Rowe was the man on rocket duty. Earlier, Rowe had seen the iceberg slip by, without realising the damage it had caused. Whilst at his post on the stern of the ship, he noticed a boat being lowered and when he rang the bridge to ask why, those on the bridge were surprised to find that he had not been informed of what had happened. After Rowe had been made aware of the situation, he was ordered to the bridge and told to bring the rockets with him. He turned up with a box containing twelve large rockets, which Smith asked about as soon as the quartermaster reached the bridge. When Rowe showed him the box the captain told him, 'Fire one, and fire one every five or six minutes.'

Rowe got ready to do so and at about 12.35 a.m., he set up the first rocket on the starboard side of the bridge, lit the taper and watched the rocket soar skywards. It burst high above the ship with a muffled thud and exploded into a bright shower of white stars that momentarily illuminated the whole scene.

Aboard the S.S. Californian, at about 12.45 a.m., Second Officer Stone saw a rocket burst above the strange ship whose lights were visible to the south. All night a series of officers and crewmen had observed the lights of a ship which had approached the ice field and stopped before it at about 11.40 p.m. Captain Lord had been one of the observers, as too had Groves, the watch officer who thought that the vessel was a passenger steamer, though Lord did not agree and nor did Stone, who had come on duty just before midnight. Stone had met Lord by the wheelhouse, where Lord had pointed out the mystery steamer to the south and told Stone to inform him if the ship started to come towards them. Lord had added that he was going for a lie-down on the settee in the chart room. Once on the bridge, Stone had more chance to look at the ship and from what he could observe, he took her to be a tramp steamer. Rather than a blaze of lights, he could distinguish only one masthead light, a few small lights on her decks and her red navigation light, which meant that the ship he saw was facing the other direction from the Titanic. But the rockets caused a buzz of interest when they started bursting above the mystery ship. Earlier attempts to contact the vessel with the Morse lamp had been useless and no-one on the Californian wished to wake up Evans, the wireless operator. Stone watched five rockets burst before he informed his captain. Lord asked if the rockets were private signals (i.e. between vessels that carried no wireless, as there were still many that did not). Stone replied that he did not know, so Lord advised him to try again with the Morse lamp.

This was equally unsuccessful. Three more rockets burst in the night sky, the last one at about 1.40. At 2 a.m., the strange ship appeared to be making off to the southwest. When he was informed of this, Lord again asked about the colour of the rockets and again urged Stone to use the Morse lamp. However, at some time between 2 a.m. and 2.20, the mysterious ship vanished completely.

Back on the Titanic, the blasé humour that had characterised the proceedings thus far then took on a far different nature as the first rockets went up. Some of the spectators were delighted at the free firework show, while others were profoundly worried. The boats had all been lowered level with the boat deck by this time and the officers were calling for the women and children. Since Smith had given Lightoller his orders to start the evacuation, most of the passengers had been roused from their cabins. For the first-class passengers it had been a polite knock on the door that had brought the stewards and stewardesses into their rooms; they had then courteously asked the passengers to please put on their life preservers (now known as life jackets) and go up onto the boat deck. In second class, the stewards had merely opened the cabin doors and told the occupants to dress and put on their life preservers.

The third-class, steerage passengers were roused in a similar manner, though many of them had already guessed that something was wrong on the ship. Those in the bow who had felt the impact, or jumped out of bed onto a wet floor, needed no further warning. At the stern of the ship, though, there were problems, as many there did not realise that anything had happened and for those who could not speak English, of whom there were many, the situation was even more confusing. There were a couple of White Star translators, but they had their work cut out and found that, as in first class, many of the passengers refused to believe that the ship was in any real danger. Also, many of the steerage passengers were not prepared to leave their luggage, which for most was all they had in the world. There was another problem for these poor people: as the first and second-class passengers were being ushered towards the boat deck, the third-class passengers found that many of the barriers that separated their decks from the upper decks had not been opened and formerly helpful stewards, without orders from above, all too often became petty officials, barring the way to the boat deck.

The best view in third class from the poop deck – perhaps the best view of any third-class passenger – was that of August Wennerstrom, a Swede whose memoirs were only recently brought to light by Titanic researcher, Wyn Craig Wade. Wennerstrom and five travelling companions from Sweden had got up and gone straight to the steerage smoking room under the poop deck. There they tried to get something to drink, but they found that the bar was closed. So, as there was nothing else to do, the passengers got somebody to play the piano and people started dancing. Nobody had any idea of what was happening and as of yet, no-one had come to tell them what to do. However, there were some people who were more nervous than the rest, the largest group being about 50 Italians who suddenly came in dressed in their life preservers, carrying their belongings in bundles on their backs. They acted as if they were crazy, leaping up and down and calling on their Madonna. Wennerstrom, a staunch Protestant, disliked seeing such expressions of religious fervour. Nobody took any serious notice of them, though – the dancers least of all, who formed a ring and danced in a circle around them.

Elizabeth Shutes was among the passengers by then moving slowly towards the boat deck. She had only had time to throw on a coat and skirt and put slippers on her feet before the stewardess had appeared with their life preservers. She and the Grahams had put these on and had been in the process of lacing them up when Mr. Roebling, another first-class passenger, with whom they were acquainted, had arrived and offered to escort them up to the boat deck.

They went past the palm room, where only a few hours earlier they had all enjoyed a concert, surrounded by a crowd of happy, smiling faces. Now everything was so different. Pale-faced stewards with armfuls of life preservers stood by the stairways, while passengers were quietly, nervously and sometimes tearfully strapping the preservers around themselves.

On the boat deck, disgruntled and sleepy first and second-class passengers were already gathering in loose bunches, waiting in the cold as Lightoller and his fellow officers began swinging out the first lifeboats. Smith's orders had by then become general and boats were being made ready for loading on either side of the ship. The officers were instructed that the evacuation was to be conducted in an orderly manner, with 'women and children first', in true Birkenhead style, but from where they got this order is unclear. Certainly Lightoller denied having received the command from Smith himself and said that he was following his own sense of humanity.

The passengers had seen Smith moving around the ship since not long after the Titanic had stopped. Shortly after midnight, Marian Thayer had been on the boat deck, from where she had caught sight of the captain giving orders on the port side of the bridge. Shortly afterwards, Martha Stevenson and Elizabeth Eustis had come to the iron stairs that led up to the forward boat deck. There they had met the captain waiting anxiously at the top of the stairs, with a worried set to his face. Nonetheless, Smith had waited courteously until the two sisters had come up the stairs before he had gone down. Now, as Lightoller was lowering boat no. 4, Smith was by his side.

He ordered Lightoller to start loading the passengers from the promenade deck, which was the one below the boat deck. Smith must have felt that this would make things easier for the women and children, rather than having them scrambling into the craft from the exposed boat deck. An expectant crowd had gathered, ready to get into the boat, but this new order was passed along to them and they all went below. However, it seems that Smith was confusing the Titanic with his old command, the Olympic, and had forgotten that the promenade deck on this new vessel was fully glazed, whereas it was open on the older ship. First-class passenger Hugh Woolner realised the mistake and said,

'Haven't you forgotten, sir, that all those glass windows are closed?'

'By God, you're right!' Smith exclaimed. 'Call those people back.'

The passengers duly came back, only to find that in the meantime their boat had been lowered to the deck below as instructed. Smith had moved on and Lightoller decided that rather than raising the boat, the windows on the promenade deck could be cranked open, so again the passengers were ordered below. Marian Thayer, worn out with all this trooping up and down, exclaimed: 'Tell us where to go and we will follow. You ordered us up here and now you are taking us back.'

Below decks in the engine room, the situation was getting worse. Even before the boats were being filled and the rockets launched, the first few casualties were being sustained. Leading Fireman Fred Barratt, who earlier had barely escaped from boiler room no. 6, was chatting to engineers Harvey and Shepherd, while others were rushing around them carrying pump hoses, in a room by then soaked more from the steam of the damped-down boilers than from the flood water. The atmosphere was one of concerted, noisy activity and because of this, the men had to be careful that they did not hurt themselves. Engineer Shepherd was unlucky and soon suffered an accident, when he fell down a service manhole and broke his leg. Barratt, Harvey and others carefully lifted him out and, to keep him out of harm's way, placed him in the pump room, a safe area at the end of the boiler room. There, they made sure that he was settled before they returned to the boiler room, which was full of the noises of men shouting, the steady whirr of the pump generators and the hiss of the pipes.

Presently, someone shouted from above that the men were to report to their boat stations. Most of the workers left, but Barratt,

Harvey and the immobilised Shepherd remained in the pump room. After another fifteen minutes, the men were fairly pleased. The pumps were working well and the floor of boiler room no. 5 was by then dry. Suddenly, though, preceded by an ominous rumble and the squeal of tortured metal, the whole bulkhead separating compartments 5 and 6 collapsed with a roar and the water surged in an angry wave along the avenue of boilers from the forward end of the ship. Harvey screamed at Barratt to get out as the water hit them, nearly bowling them over. Barratt scrambled up an escape ladder while Harvey made a vain effort to rescue Shepherd and tried to fight his way to the pump room. As Barratt got out, he lost sight of Harvey who vanished under the tide of rising water.

Second-class passenger Lawrence Beesley was by then in the second-class smoke room, where he had been since shortly after the ship had stopped. The smoke room was barely occupied – there were only a small number of the die-hard, late-night gamblers in there still playing a few hands. In an off-hand manner, some of them informed Beesley that they had seen an iceberg go by – their estimates of its size differing from 60 to 100 feet. No-one there seemed particularly interested in it, except for one of the players, who, hearing that there was ice on the boat deck, asked if there was any he could put in his whisky! To Beesley, the passengers seemed so confident aboard the Titanic, feeling as safe in her as if they were standing on a rock. Unperturbed when the ship had stopped and equally disinterested when, with a wail, the boiler relief pipes had let off steam, the passengers did, however, become more animated when the first rockets went off. Beesley found himself musing grimly that the rockets meant only one thing – the Titanic was injured badly enough to need help from any ship near enough to see her.

A strange note of urgency sounded in Beesley's mind shortly after this, about an hour after the collision, when he saw one of the Titanic's bandsmen running down the starboard side of the ship pulling behind him his cello, with its spike dragging on the deck. Bandmaster Wallace Hartley, formerly of the Cunard Line, was mustering his men for their own famous showdown. The ship's orchestra was actually formed of two groups of musicians, which may account for the varying reports about what they played that night. The orchestra had been performing on the first-class stairwell, their intention no doubt being to keep panic to a minimum. Music soothes, so it is said, and they struck up a series of cheerful, popular ragtime tunes which they carried on playing after transferring to the promenade deck. There they carried on playing their music until the angle of the deck grew so pronounced as to make any effort impossible. Why they did what they did, whether, for instance, they were following orders, remains a mystery, but in the wake of the disaster their deeds raised their names to almost cult status.

Meanwhile, Smith toured the lines of lowered boats. What originally had been only a handful of passengers gathered on the boat deck had grown into crowds which he helped to supervise, even lending a hand when some of them were a bit difficult. He came across one passenger, a Mrs. Compton, who was getting into her life preserver. Smith smiled at her and said cheerfully, 'They will keep you warm if you don't have to use them.'

The male passengers tried to be reassuring and made light of the situation whilst helping the female passengers and children into the boats. Many of the single or unaccompanied women were helped by men who had offered their services for the journey – such a courtesy was commonplace in those days – and the women were ushered to the boats by these swains. Colonel Archibald Gracie had several women under his protection, though in the crowds, search as he tried, he could find none of them and the women were safely put into the boats without him. One of these was Mrs. Churchill Candee, a thoroughly robust-looking woman, but one whom most unattached men wanted to protect. She was found by another of her table companions, Edward Kent, to whom she gave an ivory miniature of her mother for safekeeping. They were presently joined by Hugh Woolner and Bjornstrom Steffanson, another first-class passenger, and all three men helped her to boat no. 6.

Nearby, Mrs. Graham, her daughter, Margaret, and Elizabeth Shutes were ushered into boat no. 8 by Howard Case and W.A. Roebling. Later, when the boat was being lowered, the two men were still nearby. Case, displaying some nonchalant grace, carelessly lit a cigarette and stood smoking it.

In third class the chivalry continued. Katie Gilnagh, a pretty fifteen-year old, was woken by a young man who had earlier caught her eye. In another cabin, a young Finnish girl, Anna Sjoblom, was sharing with another girl and was awakened by a young Dane who had come in to wake up her roommate. He handed them both a life preserver, but Anna, being prone to seasickness, was too ill to put it on. Only after some time, when the commotion outside made her even more sick through worry, did Anna get up out of her bunk and she somehow managed to find her way to the boat deck, where an old school friend helped her into a lifeboat.

Married couples too gathered uneasily on the boat deck. In second class, one of these couples was William Angle and his wife Florence. They were returning from a visit they had made to Mr. Angle's mother in Stoke. No accounts seem to exist noting their time on the Titanic, but certainly Mr. Angle saw his wife into a boat before he melted back into the crowd to await events.

Others, though, were remembered more clearly. Officers then stood by the boats and called for women and children. Few came forward at first, but as the danger grew more apparent, couples could be seen clinging together, all too often in final, parting embraces.

American newlyweds, Dan and Mary Marvin, whose wedding had been one of the first to be filmed, now parted uneasily. Dan waved his wife into her boat and called, 'It's all right, little girl – you go and I'll stay a while.'

Novelist Jacques Futrelle, a notable writer of mysteries, escorted his wife, May, to boat no. 9, but she was reluctant to leave him, which caused him to exclaim: 'For God's sake, go! It's your last chance! Go!'

First-class passenger Arthur Ryerson had to be firm with his wife: 'You must obey orders. When they say, "Women and children to the boats", you must go when your turn comes. I'll stay here with Jack Thayer – we'll be all right.'

Smith, armed with a ship's megaphone, appeared near Mr. and Mrs. Lucien Smith when they were having a similar argument.

Seeing the captain nearby, Mrs. Smith turned to him as judge and jury and asked him if her husband could join her in the lifeboat. The captain either did not hear her or chose not to and raising his megaphone, he shouted, 'Women and children first!'

Mr. Smith interceded: 'Never mind, Captain, about that; I'll see she gets into the boat.' He then turned to his wife and spoke to her quietly and slowly: 'I never expected to ask you to obey, but this is one time you must. It is only a matter of form to have women and children first. The ship is thoroughly equipped and everyone on her will be saved.'

Mrs. Smith asked him if he was telling her the truth. He lied. 'Yes,' he said, and kissed his wife goodbye before escorting her to the boat. He then stood there watching her as the boat was lowered down towards the sea. 'Keep your hands in your pockets; it is very cold weather,' he said.

Other women, though, were not persuaded. Mrs. Hudson J. Allison saw her maid and baby son Trevor into a boat, but then clung ferociously to her husband, refusing to leave him. Also with them was their three-year old daughter, Lorraine, who hung onto her mother's skirt and was destined to be the only first-class child to die on the ship.

Ida Straus refused to be parted from her husband Isidor, the owner of the famous Macy chain of stores. Instead, she wrapped her fur coat around her maid, climbed out of the boat and rejoined Isidor on the deck, saying, 'I've always stayed with my husband, so why should I leave him now?'

Colonel Gracie, who was with them, said that he was sure that an old gentleman like Mr. Straus would be allowed to go in the boat with his wife and he was preparing to ask Lightoller when Straus proudly affirmed that he would not go before the other men. The Straus's then got out of everybody else's way by retiring to a couple of steamer chairs, where they awaited the end in each other's company.

1. THE POTTERIES IN THE NINETEENTH CENTURY.

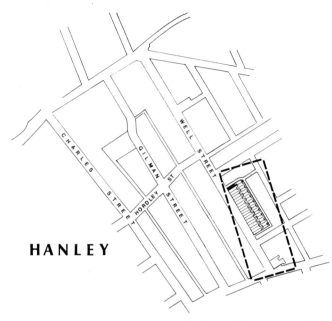

HANLEY

2. PART OF THE WELLINGTON HOUSING ESTATE IN HANLEY.
The outlined area shows the small portion of Well Street that still
exists. No. 51, where Captain Smith was born, is marked in black.

3. THE REMAINS OF WELL STREET, HANLEY. NO. 51 IS THE TOP HOUSE.

5. THE FORMER ETRURIA BOARD SCHOOL.

4. THE WESLEYAN CHAPEL, ETRURIA.

7. THE NASMYTH STEAM HAMMER.

6. THE WRECK OF THE BIRKENHEAD, a story rendered by Alfred Smith.

8. THE S.S. CELTIC.

9. THE S.S. BRITANNIC.

10. THE S.S. REPUBLIC.

11. ELEANOR SMITH.

12. ST. OSWALD'S CHURCH, WINWICK

13. CAPTAIN SMITH, dressed in his Royal Naval Reserve lieutenant's uniform.

14.   THE S.S. CUFIC.

15.   THE S.S. ADRIATIC.

16. THE S.S. GERMANIC.

17. THE S.S. MAJESTIC.

18. CHARLES HERBERT LIGHTOLLER.

19. WILLIAM T. STEAD.

21. J. BRUCE ISMAY.

20. THE S.S. BALTIC.

22. CAPTAIN SMITH CONDUCTING AN INSPECTION ON THE NEW S.S. ADRIATIC c. 1909.

23.   THOMAS ANDREWS.

24.   THE R.M.S. OLYMPIC.

25. CAPTAIN SMITH, dressed in his summer uniform on board the Olympic.

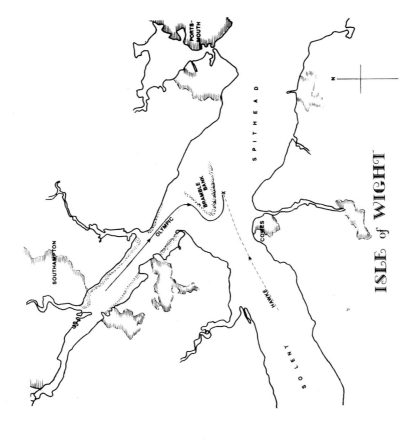

ISLE of WIGHT

27. THE LOCATION OF THE OLYMPIC - H.M.S. HAWKE INCIDENT, 20TH
SEPTEMBER 1911.

26. GEORGE BOWYER.

29. THE HAWKE AFTER THE COLLISION
WITH THE OLYMPIC.

28. DAMAGE SUSTAINED BY THE OLYMPIC IN THE
COLLISION WITH THE HAWKE.

30. MORGAN ROBERTSON.

"OLYMPIC" class liners.

STARBOARD

PORT

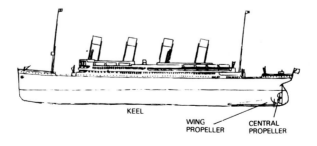

31. THE BASIC STRUCTURE OF THE OLYMPIC CLASS LINERS.

32.   THE R.M.S. TITANIC IN DOCK AT SOUTHAMPTON.

33. THE TITANIC'S À LA CARTE RESTAURANT.

34. THE TITANIC'S FIRST-CLASS SMOKING ROOM.

35. A FIRST-CLASS STATEROOM ON THE TITANIC.

36. THE TITANIC'S SECOND-CLASS LIBRARY.

37. CAPTAIN SMITH STANDING ON THE BRIDGE OF THE TITANIC.

38. CAPTAIN SMITH (front row, second from the right) AND OFFICERS OF THE TITANIC.

39.   THE TITANIC - NEW YORK INCIDENT, 10TH APRIL 1912.

40.   THE TITANIC AT QUEENSTOWN, 11TH APRIL 1912.

41. FIRST OFFICER MURDOCH.

42. FOURTH OFFICER BOXHALL.

43. SIXTH OFFICER MOODY.

44. JACK PHILLIPS AND HAROLD BRIDE.

45. FREDERICK FLEET.

46. CHARLES JOUGHIN.

47. SIR COSMO DUFF GORDON.

48. COLONEL ARCHIBALD GRACIE.

49. LAWRENCE BEESLEY.

50. AUGUST WENNERSTROM.

51. THE TITANIC'S COLLISION WITH AN ICEBERG, 11.40 P.M., 14TH APRIL 1912.

52. THE ICEBERG.

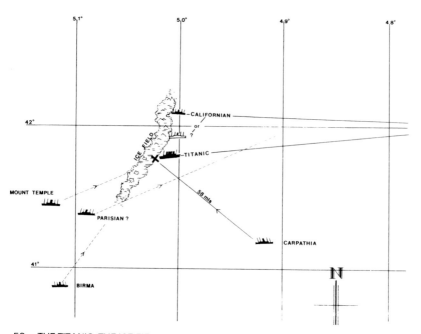

53. THE TITANIC, THE ICE FIELD AND SHIPS IN THE VICINITY, 14TH – 15TH APRIL 1912.

54. FIRST OFFICER MURDOCH GIVES CAPTAIN SMITH THE BAD NEWS.

55. CAPTAIN ARTHUR ROSTRON.

56.   THE CARPATHIA.

57.   CAPTAIN STANLEY LORD.

58.   THE CALIFORNIAN.

59.   THE TITANIC'S BAND PLAYING ON.

60. CAPTAIN SMITH EXHORTING PASSENGERS AND CREW TO 'BE BRITISH' — THE LEGEND THAT NEVER WAS

61. THE TITANIC STARTING TO SINK.

62. THE TITANIC SINKING.

63. A POSTCARD SHOWING CAPTAIN SMITH SAVING A CHILD.

64. LIFEBOAT 14 AND COLLAPSIBLE D APPROACHING THE CARPATHIA.

65. CROWDS WAITING FOR NEWS OUTSIDE THE WHITE STAR LINE'S OFFICES IN SOUTHAMPTON.

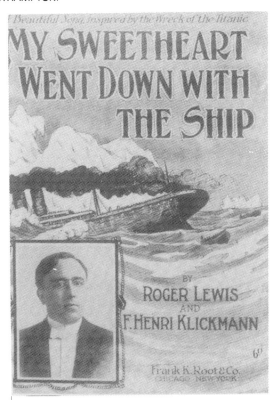

66. THE FRONT PAGE OF THE "MY SWEETHEART WENT DOWN WITH THE SHIP" SHEET MUSIC.

67. SOLDIERS COLLECTING FOR A TITANIC MEMORIAL.

68. THE STATUE OF CAPTAIN SMITH
UNVEILED BY HELEN MELVILLE SMITH,
29TH JULY 1914.

70. THE PLAQUE TO CAPTAIN SMITH IN HANLEY TOWN HALL BEING ADMIRED BY DESCENDANT, MIDSHIPMAN W. RUSSELL-SMITH.

69. THE STATUE OF CAPTAIN SMITH.

7

We Are The Titanic, Sinking

The boats were lowered from about 12.45 a.m. onwards, with the first being boat no. 7 on the starboard side of the ship. The boat's capacity was for 65 people, but it was launched with only 28 aboard. At this time still not enough people were convinced that the vessel was in any real danger, despite the urgent efforts of the ship's officers to get them into the boats.

Another problem for those lowering the boats was that there were not enough sailors to crew them. Major Arthur Peuchen, the vice-president of the Royal Canadian Yacht Club, was with a group of men watching as boat no. 6 was being winched into position on the port side. Nearby were Smith and Lightoller, one of whom called to the men, 'We must get these masts and sails out of these boats; you might give us a hand.' The men evidently helped for soon they were aiding the women and children over the short gap into the boat and shortly the craft was full. Interestingly enough, the two crewmen on this boat were Fred Fleet, who had spotted the iceberg, and Quartermaster Hitchens, who had been at the helm at the time, but neither was an experienced sailor. Mrs. Churchill Candee heard one of them call out as the boat was being lowered, 'Captain, we have no seamen.'

On deck, Smith grabbed a boy by the arm and said, 'Here's one,' and sent him down into the boat. However, he was found to be injured, so when the boat was further down, a woman's voice was heard calling out that they did not have enough men to sail the vessel.

Lightoller looked around. Nearby stood the group of male passengers to whom he called out, 'Any seamen there?'

'If you like, I will go,' said Major Peuchen stepping forward.

'Are you a seaman?'

'I am a yachtsman.'

'If you're sailor enough to get out on that fall, you can go down,' said Lightoller.

Smith, who was standing off to one side, suggested an alternative way into the boat:

'You had better go down below and break a window and get in through the window into the boat.'

Major Peuchen did not think this feasible and instead leapt the short distance to the extended rope-fall and shinned his way down from the lighted deck into the darkness of the side of the ship.

Already in boat no. 6 was Molly Brown, who earlier had been thrown to the floor of her cabin when the iceberg crashed past her window. She was one of the most colourful people aboard the Titanic and seemingly totally fearless. She had earlier helped some of the other women into their life preservers and then into their boats, never once considering that she should do the same. When she had finished she had decided to go and see what was happening elsewhere, when suddenly she had been grabbed from behind and dropped into boat no. 6, which was in the process of being lowered. She then saved the boat by fending it off from the Titanic with an oar, when water gushing from a D deck porthole threatened to submerge it. It was at that point that she looked up and caught sight of the resigned countenance of Smith, with whom she had crossed the Atlantic twice before, the last time being only three months previously on board the Olympic. Smith peered down at the people in the boat and directed the crew to make for the light in the distance whilst keeping the boats together.

Due to the lack of men in the boat, many of the women lifted the oars into the oarlocks and started off with a steady stroke. In charge of the boat, and not letting anyone forget it, was Quartermaster Hitchens, whose subsequent behaviour was to make the night in boat no. 6 nerve-wracking in the extreme. First he bawled at Major Peuchen, then fell to shouting at the women. This cavalier attitude, plus his refusal to return to the scene after the Titanic had sunk, later found the quartermaster having to answer some rather strongly-worded questions. Molly Brown took a particularly fierce dislike to the man and eventually when his

110

behaviour became unbearable, she threatened to throw him overboard. Hitchens quietened down after this outburst; Mrs. Brown, in the meantime, organised the women into bands of rowers and ended up virtually running the boat.

After watching boat no. 6 descend, Smith moved on. Alfred Crawford, a first-class steward, was assigned to crew boat no. 8, also on the port side, and was helping to load the passengers, when he noticed Smith appear on the scene just before the boat was lowered at 1.10 a.m. The Countess of Rothes, one of the passengers who escaped in boat no. 8, also noticed Smith, who stood next to her as she waited to enter the vessel. She heard him tell Tom Jones, another of the crewmen in the boat, to row 'straight for those ship's lights over there, leave the passengers aboard and return as soon as possible.'

Alfred Crawford's version was similar. He saw Smith point to a couple of lights to the north and heard him say, 'Pull for that vessel, land your people and return to the ship.'

Tom Jones, an able seaman, remembered that Smith asked him whether the plug was in the boat and Jones answered, 'Yes, sir.'

'All right,' said Smith, 'any more ladies?' And he shouted twice more, 'Any more ladies?'

Then the captain and Chief Officer Wilde supervised the lowering of the boat. Smith ordered Crawford into it, then the captain and another steward began to lower the forward falls and boat no. 8 slowly descended towards the sea. It only contained 28 people. The Countess of Rothes took the tiller. Tom Jones said of her, 'She had a lot to say and I put her to steering the boat.' However, their mutual admiration was later made clear; the countess remembered Jones as an excellent sailor, while Jones later had the numeral "8" removed from the lifeboat, framed it and sent it to the countess as a token of his esteem.

Everything was very calm. The passengers waited in crowds near to the boats and most were well-behaved. The men escorted their wives and children up to the boats, where there were tearful partings, lingering last kisses and words of comfort, but there was no disorder. Therefore, Lightoller felt that it was a waste of valuable time when Wilde asked him to find the ship's firearms. Lightoller led

Wilde, Smith and First Officer Murdoch to the locker where the weapons were kept and handed out one apiece. The guns were to be used in the event of panic.

However, no such general panic seemed ready to materialise. Smith tucked the gun into his pocket and returned to the bridge, where he stood watching Boxhall and Rowe firing off the rockets. Boxhall was rather stunned by the events. The overall lack of panic and any of the violence usually associated with terrible disasters seemed even then to make him doubt that the ship was in any real danger.

'Captain, is it really serious?' he asked.

'Mr. Andrews tells me that he gives her from an hour to an hour and a half,' Smith replied quietly.

In that hour and a half left to them, some people did extraordinary things. Baker, Charles Joughin, helped with the boats before he returned to his quarters where he slowly got drunk on a bottle of whisky. Journalist and spiritualist, W. T. Stead, retired to the first-class smoking room, picked up a book and settled himself down for a good read. First-class passenger, Edith Russell, returned to her cabin for a precious item, just one thing – a small, musical lucky pig, that played the tune "Maxixe" when its tail was turned. President Taft's aide, Major Archie Butt, joined some friends for an impromptu card game. Multimillionaire, Ben Guggenheim, discarded the warm sweater and life preserver that a steward had advised him to wear and instead he and his secretary dressed in full dinner suits and later went on deck. Mr. Guggenheim made it clear that they intended to go down like gentlemen.

At 12.30 a.m., the order had come down to the third-class stewards to begin sending up the women and children from steerage. Third-class steward, John Hart, did his best. From midnight he had been attempting to get the passengers into their life preservers, despite having to contradict what he was saying by assuring everyone that they were in no immediate danger, a reassuring comment that could not be understood by the many non-English speaking passengers, whose confusion was making them jumpy. Hart was stationed on the main third-class stairwell on E deck, which became a noisy, milling bottleneck. The barriers that should have been opened to help the evacuation of the third class to the boat deck had remained closed and Hart realised that he would have trouble getting his people up to the boats. Nonetheless, he decided personally to escort small groups and soon started off with his first party, leading them around by a complex route along corridors and the few open companionways until finally they reached the main staircase up to the boat deck. Once they were there, Hart escorted his party over to boat no. 8, only to find that many felt it was too cold and jumped out of the boat to return indoors to the warmth. Hart had to go back for more.

Others avoided the bottleneck. Some of the more adventurous passengers swarmed along the ship's cranes like lines of ants, dropping onto the upper decks at the end of their climb. Still more forced their way through the locked barriers. Katie Gilnagh and two other girls were lucky enough to be escorted by a large brawny Irish youth, who, when he found a sailor stubbornly refusing to open a gate, bawled at him so ferociously that the man instantly obeyed and opened the barrier, letting them all through.

Such an instance as this seems to confirm the popular idea that there was a mass conspiracy by the crew to keep back the third-class passengers, but this does not appear to have been the case. During the later American inquiry into the disaster, Senator William Alden Smith questioned several steerage passengers from the Titanic in relation to stories that were being carried by the press of armed officers gunning down passengers, of barriers being closed and passengers being beaten up to stop them getting to the boat deck. One story even had Smith firing a revolver into an unruly crowd of Italians! But try as he might, the senator could not elicit any real complaints from any third-class passenger. The closest he came was in his questioning of the Irishman, Daniel Buckley, who said that he saw one passenger thrown down the stairs by a sailor to stop him going into first class. The crewman locked the gate before running off, but in the meantime the fallen passenger had risen and burst the lock, threatening to throw the sailor overboard if he caught him. Buckley, though, did not mean this to be a general comment on the overall conduct of the crew or to suggest that the steerage passengers were under general restraint.

'Did these passengers in steerage have any opportunity at all of getting out?' asked Senator Smith.

'Yes, they had,' said Buckley.

'What opportunity did they have?'

'I think they had as much chance as the first and second-class passengers.'

'After this gate was broken?'

'Yes.'

Olaus Abelseth's testimony at the inquiry was even more assured; there had, to his mind, been no restraint. He recalled that a gate had been shut, but was opened for the ladies and finally for the men.

'Do you think that the passengers in the steerage and in the bow of the boat had an opportunity to get out and up on the decks, or were they held back?' Senator Smith enquired.

'Yes, I think they had an opportunity to get up,' Abelseth replied.

'There were no gates or doors locked, or anything that kept them down?'

'No sir, not that I could see.'

'You were not under restraint? You were permitted to go aboard the boats the same as the other passengers?'

'Yes, sir.'

Nor does the popular image of there having been a mass panic in third class seem to be true. This legend was prompted by class prejudice and what panic there was, was no more or no less than in first or second class. The steerage passengers, who were mostly from working-class backgrounds, were seen as the uneducated "masses", a faceless cross section of foreigners and the "lower orders", whom members of the Establishment were convinced would panic at the first sign of trouble. In actuality, many of the third-class passengers awaited the end with a quiet resignation that put many of the upper classes to shame. August Wennerstrom, for instance, had all this time been only too happy to stay in the steerage smoking room and was not eager to get up to the boat deck. Instead, he was content to stand calmly smoking a cigar whilst watching the boats being lowered down the side of the ship. He noticed everything and felt nothing but an intense interest in what was going on, as if he was a member of an audience watching a marvellous dramatic play.

Wennerstrom later made no mention of people being restrained or needing to be restrained; instead he was surprised and even alarmed by the resignation with which people sat around awaiting their fate. A man named John Lundahl had recently been on a visit to his old homeland and was returning to the United States. Now he calmly said, 'Goodbye friends; I'm too old to fight the Atlantic,' before he walked into the smoking room and sat down on a chair. Then there was an English lady who sat by the piano with her child on her knee and played on the instrument at least until Wennerstrom left the room and perhaps until she died.

White Star always later denied that it was company policy to discriminate against third-class passengers and they obviously felt that they were telling the truth. As is made clear in Walter Lord's excellent book "A Night to Remember", many of the third-class passengers felt that in such a situation the first and second-class passengers should enjoy the privilege of being the first into the boats, which seems to match with Wennerstrom's observations of the curious listlessness that infected many of the third-class travellers. Steward Hart's testimony shows that there were orders passed down to get the steerage women and children up to the boats from as early as 12.30 a.m., fifteen minutes before the first boat was launched and almost two hours before the Titanic foundered. Prompt efforts were made to get them up to the boat deck and there they were treated in exactly the same manner as the wealthier passengers. The main problem was that there was so little organisation in respect of these poor people; there were too many barriers left unopened and too many crew members not prepared to take the initiative without orders from above – orders that no-one seemed to remember to give. This is borne out by the casualty figures of that night.

The starboard boats in particular saw little activity around them and the decks there were almost deserted at times. There seems to be little explanation for this other than that the people appear to have been attracted to the society and imagined security of the crowds on the port side boat deck. First Officer Murdoch supervised the loading of the starboard boats, just as Lightoller did the port boats, but Murdoch had problems finding enough women and children to fill the boats. Not surprisingly perhaps, his interpretation of the 'women and children first' order, which for men such as Lightoller meant women and children only, was far more liberal and Murdoch allowed some men to get into the boats. Lawrence Beesley from second class was one of these – he and several other male passengers got into boat no. 13, which was mostly filled with second and third-class women and children. The boat was lowered at about 1.25 a.m. with over 60 people aboard.

Beesley, like Wennerstrom in third class, was wide awake to what was happening around him and gloried a little in the sense of what a great adventure he was involved in as the boat was slowly and steadily lowered down the side of the dark hull. In his memoirs, to help to give a clear impression of his feelings, he asked the reader to measure 75 feet up the side of a tall building, then to look down from that height and imagine himself being lowered down it in a series of calculated jerks.

When boat no. 13 settled on the sea, though, its problems started. No-one knew how to release the falls and as they all dithered as to what to do, the boat was carried along the side of the ship to directly underneath another boat that was being lowered. Those in boat no. 13 shouted warnings, as too did those in the descending boat, but the men on the deck in control of the davits could not hear their cries. For a few moments it looked as though a miniature disaster would happen as the occupants of boat no. 13 seemed likely to be crushed, but a crewman found a knife with which he cut the falls and the boat got away just in time.

Once they were clear, despite the fact that 25 of those in the boat were crewmen, the passengers discovered that most of them were stokers and that they were useless at trying to control the boat. They crossed oars, banged the oars together and got nowhere. When that failed they commenced shouting at one another from either end of the boat, asking what they should do. It seemed that there was no-one in charge, so in desperation the passengers elected one of the stokers as the leader and hoped that the night ahead of them would be smoother.

WE ARE THE TITANIC, SINKING

Beesley did not recognise any of the other people on his boat, but then it was dark and he could only see a yard or two at most. However, he later guessed that there had been no first-class passengers aboard and only three women, a baby and two male passengers from second class. The other occupants were the 25 crewmen and about 35 third-class passengers, who were mostly female. Most of the starboard boats had such unusual disparities, with crewmen and a mixture of classes and sexes, compared with the virtual uniformity of the port side boats. Unlike boat no. 13 though, some of the starboard boats had gone away from the ship virtually empty. One of these had been emergency boat no. 1, which had left the Titanic with only 12 people aboard, mostly crew and a small knot of first-class passengers, the most notable of whom were Sir Cosmo Duff Gordon and Lady Duff Gordon with her maid. When the boat had been swung out, Murdoch had been unable to find any women and children up at that end of the ship, which was just behind the bridge. So, when the Duff Gordon party showed up and asked if they could go in, he politely allowed them into the boat. When some crewmen and a few other male passengers appeared, they too went in. Murdoch must then have lowered the boat with so few aboard, believing that it would return to pick up swimmers after the ship had sunk. However, this never happened and Lord Duff Gordon later encountered a storm of controversy when he was asked to explain some of his actions that night.

On the bridge, Smith's mind was still on the light to the north, which seemed sometimes to come towards them, sometimes to stop and at other times to retreat. Boxhall had tried unsuccessfully to contact the vessel with the Morse lamp, so he moved on to his boat station. Quartermaster Rowe was still there, however, and Smith asked him if he knew Morse. Rowe replied that he knew some and Smith said, 'Call that ship up and when she replies, tell her, "We are the Titanic sinking; please have all your boats ready."'

Rowe got to work and when he was not firing the distress rockets, he flashed out the message over and over again, but there was still no response. After a little time, Rowe thought that he could see another light on the horizon, off the starboard quarter. When he informed his captain, Smith raised his binoculars and studied the light, but he informed Rowe presently that it was just a star low on the horizon. At least Rowe was being alert; Smith smiled and handed the young quartermaster his binoculars so that he could see for himself.

By then many of the boats had gone. At about 1.15, the water had been up to about C deck and the people in the boats were shocked to see how low the Titanic was in the water. The sea lapped over the name "TITANIC" on the bow and soon after, the prow finally vanished under the sea and water began to inch its way up the forecastle. The Titanic's band was still playing its airy ragtime tunes, the sound of which could be heard in some of the nearest lifeboats. From their viewpoint, the Titanic, lit up like a Christmas tree, lay dying in a sea that hardly seemed able to muster a light wave. Deep inside the ship the engineers were still drawing the boilers, even though cold water sloshed around their knees. More men worked dragging hoses the length of the still unflooded compartments. Chief Engineer Bell had ordered that all the watertight doors aft of compartment no. 4 were to be opened to facilitate this; each door could be closed as the men retreated. In the wireless room, Phillips was still tapping away, while Bride was employed shuttling messages to the bridge.

Smith moved back and forth between the deck and the bridge, with brief visits to the wireless room to warn the operators that the power was failing, that the Titanic had not long to go and that the sea was in the engines. Phillips was by then almost begging ships to come to them. At 1.45, he pleaded desperately to the Carpathia, 'Come as quickly as possible, old man; engine room filling up to the boilers.'

The Carpathia was making her best speed and thundered through the water, with all her internal heating off, her public rooms converted into makeshift hospitals and lights and lines fastened to her side. Her officers had never known such a headlong chase.

The Titanic, meanwhile, was having further difficulties. Unbalanced by the flood waters and the mass of people on the port side, the ship began losing equilibrium. By 1.40, this grew so pronounced that Chief Officer Wilde ordered everybody over to the starboard side of the ship to get her back on an even keel.

It was at about this time that collapsible boat C on the starboard side was put into its davits and made ready for loading. Wilde was on hand to supervise the loading of this boat, but before he commenced he called out, asking who was in charge of the craft. Nearby on the bridge, Smith heard him and turning to young Quartermaster Rowe, who was still using the Morse lamp, ordered him to go. Rowe went as told and hopped into the boat.

Standing near to the boat was J. Bruce Ismay. Ismay had begun the night in a mild panic, frantically urging the passengers to get to their boats, until Fifth Officer Lowe shouted at him and told him to get out of his way. Since then, though, Ismay had behaved creditably, helping the women and children into the boats, and no-one could fault his steadiness. Now he stood watching collapsible boat C being filled, but when no-one else came forward and the boat began to be lowered, Ismay stepped into it and sat down. It was a move that was to haunt him for the rest of his life.

Boat no. 4 on the port side had been the first boat swung out, but Lightoller had discovered that the ship's sounding spar was blocking its descent and needed to be removed, a process which took some time. In the meantime, the boat's passengers had to wait. Eleanor Widener, Marian Thayer and eventually the heavily pregnant Madelene Astor were put into the boat along with many others. Multimillionaire, J.J. Astor, escorted his young wife to the boat and due to her 'delicate condition' would have joined her but for the second officer's stern refusal. Instead, Astor said goodbye and melted back into the crowd on B deck.

The boat was finally lowered at 1.55 a.m., by which time the angle of the ship had so increased that what was usually a distance of 60 feet from the boat deck to the water had then shrunk to about 15 feet. When the small craft eventually touched down, the passengers discovered that there were not enough sailors aboard, so a quartermaster was sent down one of the falls to help.

With the departure of boat no. 4, all of the major lifeboats were away, floating at a distance, waiting for the Titanic to sink. There were by then only three of the collapsible boats for the remaining passengers. Collapsible D, on the port side situated next to boat no. 2's davits, was easily swung out and loaded. Lightoller hurried forward and worked feverishly. The sea was already high on the forecastle, churning up through C to B deck and the large, square forward ports were taking in water. The second officer cast a glance around him. As the ship's nose had settled, most of the passengers had moved astern, but he still had work to do. The collapsible boat was rigged up and a crowd formed around it instinctively. Earlier, Lowe had had to fire warning shots to bring an unruly crowd to its senses when they tried to rush a boat. But Lightoller took another, less drastic course of action and had crew members lock arms around collapsible D, while he asked for the women and children to come forward from what passengers were still nearby. "Mr. Hoffman" handed over his two kidnapped young sons. Theatre manager Henry B. Harris escorted his wife to the circle and stepped back. Emily Goldsmith and her son, Frank, tearfully said goodbye to Frank Goldsmith Snr. before getting into the boat. More followed after them and soon the boat was filled. The sound of breaking crockery below greeted the boat as at 2.05 it was lowered the short distance to the sea, at which point first-class passengers Hugh Woolner and Bjornstrom Steffanson decided to jump for it and landed uncomfortably in the craft, the last to leave the Titanic in the usual way.

Shortly after collapsible D reached the water, millionaire Frederick M. Hoyt swam up to the boat and was taken on board. Only a short time earlier he had been talking with Smith. He had known Smith for fifteen years, but his final conversation with him did not amount to much; Hoyt did not expect to be saved and found it hard to talk. He sympathised with Smith about the accident, but he did not want to bother him with questions. Smith, however, suggested that his old friend should go to A deck to see if there was a boat alongside. This Hoyt did and to his surprise, he found collapsible D still in its davits, having been delayed in lowering. It occurred to Hoyt that if he jumped into the water, swam out and waited then he would have a chance to get into the boat. That was what he did and when the boat pulled away from the Titanic, he was soon aboard.

As the sea was gushing up the forward end of A deck at 2.05,

Phillips and Bride were still in the wireless cabin. Phillips was still stoically sending messages, the terseness of which reflected the increasingly desperate situation. It was then that Smith came in to deliver his final message to them, the order to abandon ship:

'Men, you have done your full duty,' he said quietly. 'You can do no more. Abandon your cabin. Now it's every man for himself. You look after yourselves. I release you.' There was a pause ... 'That's the way of it at this kind of time. Every man for himself.'

Then he left.

The short, truncated sentences must have showed the bitterness, fear and desolation Smith was feeling. There were none of the false heroics later ascribed to him – instead we are left with a picture of a devoted captain knowing and doing his own duty. After what "The Times" later called 'two hours of restrained heroism', Smith went around telling his crew to save themselves while they could. Fireman McGann was told, 'Well, boys, it's every man for himself.' The men working to free the boats on the officers' quarters heard him say, 'You've done your duty, boys. Now it's every man for himself.' Steward Edward Brown heard the captain call out, 'Well, boys, do your best for the women and children and look out for yourselves.' Brown then watched Smith, megaphone in hand, walk slowly back onto the bridge to await the end.

As Smith stood alone, who knows what thoughts flickered through his mind. There is a popular concept that a person's life flashes before his eyes as he is drowning – maybe thoughts of his family and home or his pet dog came to Smith. Perhaps there was an echo of his old teacher's rendering of the wreck of the Birkenhead as his mind returned to the backstreets of Hanley, his school days, old friends or his time at the forge. Perhaps snatches of a long, relatively uneventful career at sea and the honours that came with it drifted into his thoughts. Maybe in these last moments his eyes rested on the plaque that hung on the bridge, where the word "Overconfidence" was underlined in red in the White Star regulations, and perhaps he had time to revise his own views on the safety of modern ships. But whatever his last thoughts were, he took them with him. Alone on the bridge of his last command, Smith stood there looking out over the calm but killing waters that were slowly engulfing his ship.

By this time, all the major lifeboats had gone and only two collapsibles remained fixed on top of the officers' quarters either side of the forward funnel. There, Lightoller still struggled on by then minus his jacket as, despite the freezing cold temperatures, he was sweating profusely. Nearby stood a group of the ship's pursers, who, not having been assigned lifeboat duties, were just quietly waiting for the ship to sink. One of them, seeing Lightoller, piped up, 'Hello, Lights. Are you warm?' Lightoller, in admiration of their steadiness, momentarily left his duties to go over to the men and shake hands with them and they all wished one another luck.

As the sea was gurgling up the forward deck, Lightoller and his small team of men fought to unload collapsible boat B. Among the seamen was Colonel Gracie, who produced a penknife to help with the ropes. Lightoller still had hopes of getting some passengers away in the boat, but even as they were working, most of the passengers moved aft, unaware that there was still a chance of escape, and from the lifeboats, hundreds of people could be seen gathered up on the rising stern section. Among this lot were Jack Thayer and his friend Long. Thayer described the crowd as 'a mass of hopeless, dazed humanity', which may offer some explanation as to why there was no terrible panic after the last boats had gone – either everyone was stunned into a calm of disbelief or they sought consolation from a higher power. Father Thomas Byles in second class led a large crowd in prayer, after which he took over a hundred confessions. August Wennerstrom looked on with contempt:

'Hundreds were in a circle with a preacher in the middle, praying, crying, asking God and Mary to help them. They lay there still crying till the water was over their heads. They just prayed and yelled, never lifting a hand to help themselves. They had lost their own willpower and expected God to do all the work for them.'

The Titanic's band finished the last of the ragtime tunes that they had played all night, but before they laid down their instruments, they struck up one final song. Some said that it was a popular tune called "Autumn" (possibly Joyce's "Songe d'Automne", which was no. 114 in the band's repertoire), others that it was the old hymn

"Nearer My God To Thee", which is said to have been the tune that bandmaster Wallace Hartley favoured for his own funeral.

At 2.17, Jack Phillips was still in the wireless room sending out final messages. Harold Bride was ready to leave, when he looked at Phillips only to see a stoker attempting to unlace Phillips' life preserver without him noticing, but the stoker's efforts did not last for long. In a rage Bride pounced on the man and clubbed him to the floor, leaving him for dead. The struggle had finally pulled Phillips away from the wireless and the two operators rushed outside. Then, though, they went separate ways; Phillips immediately ran aft and Bride never saw him again.

Thomas Andrews, who had earlier signed the ship's death warrant and effectively started the evacuation, had spent his last hours helping the women and children into the boats and telling stewardesses to wear their life preservers so as to encourage the passengers to do so. Then, though, he resigned himself to his own death. He retired to the first-class smoking room and enjoyed a final cigarette, with apparently no intention of trying to escape.

Mr. and Mrs. Allison, with little Lorraine, were last seen smiling on the deck. Isidor and Ida Straus were also still in each other's company, apparently ready to meet fate with dignity and grace. Baker, Charles Joughin, primed to the eyeballs on neat whisky, staggered with perfect equilibrium up the slanting poop deck. Colonel Archibald Gracie, his help with collapsible B over, found himself trapped between the retreating crowds and the rising sea water. Gracie looked towards the back of the ship in time to see hundreds of people welling up from the lower decks. Most of these were third-class passengers who in the last moments had surged up the main stairwell under the poop and Gracie never forgot the horror he felt at finding that so many women and children were still on board, when he thought they had all been put in the boats. On deck, the multimillionaires mingled with the poorest emigrants – class distinctions and prejudice were washed away in the face of their mutual peril with all of them locked for a moment in time, a moment of awful calm. Then the Titanic started her final plunge.

Lightoller and his companions, one of whom by then was Harold Bride, actually managed to get collapsible B into the water before the ship began to slide forward under the sea. Suddenly, though, the water surged up onto the men as they pushed the boat forward and Lightoller lost his grip. But the boat was away and he felt that he had done his full duty. He went to the starboard side of the ship to see if all the other boats were away – they were, as collapsible A had just been washed off the deck – then he returned to the wheelhouse and dived headfirst into the sea.

Floating free, the second officer had no idea what to do; his brain, which was already numb from the constant activity, was further confused by the shocking cold of the sea water that pierced him 'like a thousand knives being driven into one's body'. In this state, he looked for somewhere safe and all he could see was the ship's crow's nest that was still above water, towards which he instinctively swam. Luckily, though, he never made it; the Titanic, moving through the water beneath him, sucked him under and he found himself whirling in a vortex, then trapped against a ventilation grill at the base of the forward funnel, pinned there by the force of the water going down into the decks below. It seemed as though he was done for, until a blast of hot air rising from within the ship blew him free. He reached the surface gasping for air and found himself surrounded by floating bodies, but then he was pulled under again as the water poured into another air shaft. Perhaps he lost consciousness – certainly he could not clearly remember how he got away this time, but when he came to he was again on the surface and near to the boat he had fought to free, which had overturned.

As Lightoller reached collapsible B, the Titanic's superstructure began to break apart. The guy wires on the forward funnel, unable to take the strain caused by the angle that the funnel had then attained, snapped, and with a roar the funnel buckled, then ripped free of the deck and crashed down into the water, killing dozens of swimmers. Fortunately for Lightoller and the others who clutched at collapsible B, the falling funnel caused a wave that washed the boat to one side, safely out of harm's way.

Bride had helped Lightoller and his men to unload collapsible B and as the rising sea carried the boat out, Bride had hold of an oarlock, which he hung onto for dear life. When the wave from the collapsing funnel washed the boat aside, Bride went with it, trapped

124

underneath the capsized craft. He was underwater and thought that he was going to die, but somehow he managed to scramble out from beneath the boat and gasped as he burst into the open air. When he recovered his breath, Bride cast a glance back at the Titanic. Hundreds of people in their white life preservers dotted the sea around the ship, but the Titanic seemed to be everything to him –she was a beautiful sight to his young eyes, heeling up out of the water, with sparks shooting out of her funnels. Yet it was all so terrible that it seemed like the end of the world.

On the ship the water rose rapidly, forcing its way like an angry wave, rushing through and over the partially crushed bridge and officers' quarters, down into the cauldron ripped open by the crashing funnel and up the forward boat deck and the distinctive, glazed first-class promenades. The water crashed through steerage accommodation, tippled over the watertight bulkheads and swept through engine room no. 4 into no. 3 and further back, killing dozens of stokers and engineers who had no time to escape as it rushed through the innards of the ship.

It was in these last desperate moments that a few lucky souls jumped for it. Young Jack Thayer had been separated from his parents in the press of bodies on the boat deck, but unbeknownst to him, his mother had got into a lifeboat, while his father had stepped back into the crowd and went down with the ship. Thayer, in the meantime, was still with his friend Long. The ship was listing to port, but shortly after this she straightened up before beginning her gradual dive to the ocean floor, sinking into the sea at an angle of about 30°. The two friends stood by the rails about level with the second funnel and decided there and then that their best chance of survival lay in making the jump into the sea. They shook hands, said goodbye and wished each other luck then climbed over the railing. Long went first; letting go of the rail, he let himself slide down the side of the ship, but Thayer jumped away from the ship just a few seconds after Long and it was a tactic that undoubtedly saved his life as Thayer never saw Long again. He believed that by sliding down the ship, Long must have been sucked down into one of the closed decks and trapped. Thayer hit the water after a drop of ten yards and was himself sucked under for a time, but swimming for his life, he found the strength to struggle clear.

Colonel Archibald Gracie had jumped into the rising wave of water as you would jump into one at the seaside, but instead of carrying him away as the ebb of a wave should, this one still rose and deposited him on the roof of the officers' quarters. There, he clung to an iron railing until the ship began to sink away from under him, dragging him down with it. He found himself in an underwater whirlpool and was petrified that he might be boiled alive by the hot water rising from the boilers. But somehow he broke free from the suction and, swimming with 'unusual strength', he got clear and rose to the surface, with his lungs fit to burst.

Almost to the end, every light on the ship was ablaze, from portholes and upper staterooms and as high as the lonely lights on the ship's masts. Marian Thayer, in boat no. 4, watched 'tier upon tier of lights disappear beneath the water as the forward part of the ship slid down as though being launched'. But as the water climbed and reached the second funnel, the generators, where Chief Engineer Bell and his brave men must have made a last stand, were flooded. As many witnesses later testified, the ship was lit up brilliantly, filling their vision, when suddenly all the lights went out, winked back on dull and red for a moment and then went out for good. The only one that remained was a rear mast light run off a separate battery. All that could be seen of the Titanic was her dark silhouette against a navy blue night sky that was dotted with brilliant stars, which leapt out more vividly with the light from the ship having gone. The dark stern hung a full 45° out of the water, with the three massive bronze alloy propellers hanging high above the sea.

Only a brief pause followed before there was an ominous noise from deep within the ship, which Marian Thayer described as sounding like a boat being dragged across a pebbly beach. To Lightoller, clutching onto collapsible B, it was a roar, but others found it indescribable. Inside the Titanic, her 29 massive boilers had suddenly broken free from their mountings and ripped forward through the ship, followed by every loose object aboard, which fell and tumbled towards the bow. Beds, chairs, tables, lamps, crockery and fittings from the galleys, furniture from the dining rooms, the deserted mail bags, passengers' luggage, a vintage car in one of the holds, the food in the stores and the ship's pantry, rows of saucepans, drawers of cutlery, bottles of wine, presses, mirrors, baths, pictures and the contents of the ship's three libraries all lunged forward. The increased weight in the nose and the strain already placed on the Titanic then told on the frame and some witnesses thought there was an explosion, but it was the rending sound of the ship breaking to bits that they heard as, just aft of the first-class smoking room, the Titanic tore herself in two beneath the water.

As the unseen bow sank away, the stern of the ship, which was still crowded with passengers 'clinging in clusters or bunches, like swarming bees', according to Jack Thayer, seemed to begin to right itself. August Wennerstrom from steerage had managed to scramble aboard the swamped collapsible A, which had floated away from the Titanic as she sank. Now, despite the cold and being up to his knees in icy water, Wennerstrom could not take his eyes off the upended liner scarcely 50 feet away from him. As the stern rose up, the starlight cast a weird halo around it and Wennerstrom, though dumbstruck with terror, marvelled at the life and death struggle taking place before him. Even then people were making an effort to save themselves – Wennerstrom could clearly see one man climbing down the ship's log line that hung limp beside the huge rudder.

Jack Thayer was just as close, holding on to the capsized collapsible B. He watched the ship hanging at about 65°-70° for what seemed like an age. Then the stern of the ship began to slowly spin around in the water, turning the decks away as if wishing to spare Thayer the sight of the hundreds still clinging there. His boat was slowly being drawn towards the pivoting stern and presently the craft's passengers found that they were almost directly under the propellers, so Thayer was convinced that the boat would be crushed by them as they came down. The stern continued to rise, until finally it was perpendicular with the sea and stood there like an accusing finger before it gently settled back a little and finally began to sink. Slowly at first, but with increasing speed as the water began to invade the ruptured framework, the stern vanished deeper into the water. The watchers in the boats – those who could watch – were transfixed by the sight. The rear half of the Titanic's superstructure had already disappeared, but now the aft well deck and the poop deck were swallowed, followed by the propellers, the rudder and finally the last peak of the stern and the flagpole. There, Charles Joughin, undoubtedly the luckiest and drunkest man of the night, was standing atop the stern. The water rose around him and he just stepped off into the sea. As the bottom had been blown off the ship there was no suction and he later claimed he never even got his hair wet! Then the ship was gone, vanishing for good under a cloud of bubbles, with a final burst of escaping air from those famous watertight compartments.

In the lifeboats there was stunned silence. On collapsible B, as the ship vanished, someone breathed, 'She's gone!' From her more distant lifeboat, Martha Stevenson had tried not to look, but glanced up to witness the final plunge. In collapsible C, J. Bruce Ismay leant over his oar, unable to look. The time was 2.20 a.m. on Monday 15th April 1912. All that was left over from the Titanic was a motley gathering of lifeboats and hundreds of people scattered around in the swirling patch of sea where the mighty liner had gone down.

Colonel Gracie never saw the ship sink, as he had been dragged down with the forward half and only reached the surface in time to hear a loud gulp as the sea finally closed over the stern. He remembered instead the thin, grey vapour that hung like a pall a few feet above the water and the tangled wreckage. The effect seemed almost supernatural, prompting in Gracie gloomy visions of the infernal regions of Greek mythology – of Charon, the ferryman of the dead, piloting his spectral boat across the River Styx. Hanging first onto a plank, then a crate and forming ideas of building a raft, Gracie found himself surrounded by hundreds in a similar perilous situation. From all quarters were shrieks and cries from people in the water: 'Help! Help! Boat ahoy!' and 'My God! My God!'

Gracie was fortunate. Nearby was collapsible B, from which were hanging Lightoller, Jack Thayer and Harold Bride, but Gracie managed to get a place aboard the craft. The screams of those freezing to death lasted for some time, but gradually they grew weaker before fading into silence.

August Wennerstrom in collapsible A was in the thick of the survivors in the water. In a 200-foot circle around the boat were hundreds of people all crying and praying for help, swimming up to the canvas-sided craft and clinging to it until it overbalanced and Wennerstrom and the others were tipped into the water. Wennerstrom lost consciousness. When he recovered he found himself floating on top of three corpses who were linked together in death. He had lost track of time, but by then the wailing had died down and no-one stopped him as he struggled over to collapsible A. The boat was completely flooded and was being kept afloat only by the cork ring that ran around it.

His friend Edward Lindell was also in the boat, but Mrs. Lindell was missing. Wennerstrom looked around, saw her in the water and grabbed her hand, but he no longer had the strength to pull her aboard. After half an hour he lost his grip and saw her vanish beneath the sea. In shock, he turned to look at Mr. Lindell and received another jolt. At first glance his friend looked as if he had aged 60 years – his face had sunk, his hair was grey and his eyes stared straight ahead. Wennerstrom looked closer and realised that Lindell had frozen to death where he sat.

Harold Bride had eventually clambered onto collapsible B where someone sat on his feet, but he was too worn out to care. The efforts of all the men aboard the overturned boat were eventually organised by Lightoller, who, despite the numbing cold, again proved himself to be a tower of strength. The boat was slowly sinking, so Lightoller had the men standing up in a line along the keel, ordering them to lean left or right whenever the light swell shifted the boat's balance. Bobbing alongside was Charles Joughin, who had been in the water longer than most, but the alcohol in his body must have acted like antifreeze. Eventually, when one of those on the boat was found to be dead, Joughin was hauled aboard in his place. Lightoller's tactics worked and collapsible B stayed afloat until they met up with one of the proper lifeboats, which took them aboard.

August Wennerstrom and the others in collapsible A were rescued when a lifeboat rigged with sail eventually heard their calls for help. This was boat no. 14 under Fifth Officer Lowe. Later Lowe unloaded his passengers onto several other boats, then he and four volunteers rowed back to where the Titanic had gone down. Many of the other lifeboats never returned to the scene – in some the passengers protested when the crew showed signs that they were going back and argued that they would be swamped, while in others the crew themselves feared to return. There was equal blame on both sides, therefore, that over 300 people froze to death in their life preservers in the cold north Atlantic Ocean. For those that went back, though, there was little danger – Lowe's boat only managed to rescue three people, one of whom later died.

The lifeboats then drifted, having finally given up on the light on the horizon that danced before them like some will-o'-the-wisp. Instead they pulled in their oars and waited for the morning.

Close with the dawn came the Carpathia, dodging icebergs and firing rockets. The small Cunard liner had amazed her crew, but found her mercy dash rewarded with only a few lifeboats containing just under a third of the passengers and crew from the Titanic. Some of the boats that huddled up to the Carpathia in the early morning light of 15th April were still more than half-empty, while others were packed to the gunwales, having taken on survivors from the collapsibles. It had been a night that had made and broken careers, but all of that was a problem for later. Now, the survivors and their rescuers had to come to terms with the enormity of the disaster that had overtaken the 'unsinkable' Titanic, a disaster that would soon be headline news around the world. The morning roll call revealed a terrible loss of life. The Titanic had gone to sea with 35 engineers, of whom none had survived; only eight of the 305 firemen and stokers had got away; none of the teenage lift boys had survived, nor had any of the purser's department; the five postal clerks had gone; the ship's band had died to a man; whole families of passengers had been wiped out and there hundreds of widows and fatherless children. Some of the ship's officers had got away in charge of their respective boats, but Sixth Officer Moody was dead and so too were First Officer Murdoch and Chief Officer Wilde. Of the 2,227 passengers and crew who had left Queenstown aboard the Titanic but a few days before, only 705 were rescued; 1,522 people were missing, one of whom was Commander Edward John Smith.

8

A Gallant Name

Even before the Carpathia landed the survivors at New York, the demise of the Titanic was headline news around the world. Throughout the remainder of the Carpathia's journey to the United States, despite a severe case of frostbite, Harold Bride, the Titanic's sole surviving Marconi operator, helped the Carpathia's wireless man to transmit the names of survivors to anxious friends and relatives on both sides of the Atlantic. When the Carpathia arrived in New York Harbour, the ship was met by a large crowd of onlookers, relatives, police, officials, reporters and medical staff, all wanting to catch sight of the survivors and to discover more about the terrible disaster that had befallen the Titanic and cost so many lives.

Almost immediately, inquiries were called for to look into the loss of the Titanic. With the witnesses at hand (though many were anxious to move on), the American government convened the first official inquiry into the disaster. This was chaired by Senator William Alden Smith and proved in the long run to be more of a talking-shop rather than an in depth inquiry. Senator Smith and his team collected a great many first-hand accounts from survivors, but the officials' lack of seagoing knowledge often exasperated many of the officers who were questioned, especially Second Officer Lightoller, the senior surviving officer of the Titanic, who left the inquiry convinced that the whole proceedings had been a farce.

When the crew and some of the passengers returned to Britain, the British government inquiry was set up under the charge of Lord Mersey. This was more interested in the technicalities of the disaster and few witnesses were called from amongst the Titanic's survivors, so in retrospect, the two inquiries complemented each other. However, not everyone was pleased with Lord Mersey's report either, as it papered over far too many cracks in maritime procedure and struck many as a face-saving cover-up.

Despite their faults, both inquiries did agree on guidelines regarding future ship safety: wirelesses were to be manned 24 hours a day and all ships would be obliged to carry enough lifeboats for all on board. Also, the inquiries sanctioned the creation of a body to monitor the flow of ice in the north Atlantic to ensure that such an accident could never occur again. This became the International Ice Patrol, which now operates as a part of the U.S. Coastguard, and is an organisation that has been so successful since its creation in 1913 that no such incidents as befell the Titanic have since occurred in areas patrolled by it.

Aside from the technical and safety side of the inquiries, it was perhaps a strange mirror of the times that a great deal of attention was focused on the behaviour of a number of individuals. During the American inquiry for instance, J. Bruce Ismay, the White Star chairman, was given a severe mauling by the American press, which accused him of, among other things, using his influence to secure himself a place in one of the lifeboats and even of causing the disaster through exerting undue pressure on Smith to make a speedy crossing, both of which accusations were untrue. He was also questioned during the British inquiry in relation to a number of incidents, including his argument with Fifth Officer Lowe when the latter told Ismay to get out of his way. Rather than launching into a spirited defence of his position, Ismay claimed ignorance of shipping and seagoing matters, which, as he was a shipping magnate, caused widespread disbelief. However, he was treated far more leniently by the British press who seemed to have smelt a scapegoat in the making. Many of the newspapers recognised that Ismay, for the majority of his time that night, had behaved in a highly responsible and brave manner, helping the women and children into the boats. Even his outburst early in the evening was brought on by a desire to save lives. His stepping into the boat was just one moment of weakness – a natural desire to survive. Yet the scandal was something Ismay never lived down. A broken man, he shortly after this retired to Ireland, where until his death in the 1930s he lived as a virtual recluse.

A GALLANT NAME

There was also the conduct of Lord and Lady Duff Gordon, whom Murdoch had allowed into boat no. 1, which had left the Titanic virtually empty and which had never returned to the scene of the sinking. It came to light after the disaster that Sir Cosmo Duff Gordon had written out cheques for the seamen in his boat when they complained that they had lost their kits with the ship. Many people felt that this constituted a bribe to make sure that the boat never went back for fear of being swamped, but there is really little evidence to support this view. Many were also not satisfied with his escape from the Titanic, when so many women and children were left behind. This, though, as with many other aspects of the tragedy, was an argument brought on by the rather archaic social expectations of the still essentially Victorian era. Certainly no other first or second-class male passengers who were allowed into the lifeboats were treated so roughly as Duff Gordon. It was because he was a lord of the realm, if anything, that prompted many accusations. Many asked that if American multimillionaires could go down with the ship and die with dignity, why could not a British lord? Duff Gordon, often presented as a rather hard-nosed character in some accounts of the disaster, was deeply upset by the events after the catastrophe and was never quite the same as before his escape from the Titanic.

Then there was Captain Stanley Lord of the Californian. Surely, people asked, his ship was that seen from the Titanic? Surely it was the Titanic that his officers saw firing rockets? His was perhaps the hardest case to answer and certainly he was the only one censured by both inquiries for not going to the rescue of the Titanic. Since then, Titanic enthusiasts and historians have been split over whether Lord was negligent on the night in question and the captain of the Californian has gained a strong group of supporters, known collectively as "Lordites", who are not happy with many of the inconsistencies in the stories from those on the Titanic and those on the Californian. There is still a significant body of opinion that Lord was merely a convenient scapegoat for the Establishment.

The question of class preference also raised its head. Of the men, women and children on the Titanic, 63% were saved from first class and 42% from second class, but only 25% of the steerage passengers survived. Those who support the conspiracy theory put this down to the restraint of the third-class passengers by order of Captain Smith, who feared a general panic. But this goes against the statements of the steward Hart, Olaus Abelseth and Daniel Buckley and the memoirs of August Wennerstrom, all of which said that there was no restraint and certainly no pattern of restraint – just great confusion and general resignation. This isn't to say that the third-class passengers brought about their own deaths, for there were villains in this piece which were far more important.

Firstly, there was the legend of the 'unsinkable' Titanic which seems to have infected everyone, from the highest to the lowest, and caused a general disbelief when disaster struck. Worse, though, were the powerful ideologies of the nineteenth century social systems, wherein deference was paid to the upper classes at all times. The Titanic with its three tiers – rich at the top, poor at the bottom – epitomised this system and inherited its faults and prejudices. It was a system that was radically altered by the cross-class carnage of World War One, but the Titanic disaster was perhaps the first instance to reveal the faults in the structure and stand as the most awful condemnation of a hierarchical class system. Before the Titanic, nobody had been given any comparable event terrible enough to question the rights and the wrongs of the class system, but after the disaster, the privileged minority never had things so easy again.

Fair or unfair, the Titanic disaster had its villains, but at the same time it also had its heroes: the engineers; the band; the Straus's; Guggenheim and Astor; Captain Rostron of the Carpathia, who was subsequently awarded the Congressional Medal of Honour by the United States; Thomas Andrews, smoking his final cigarette; Jack Phillips, sticking to his wireless until the end, and Captain Smith. As was the custom at that time because he was not there to offer evidence in his defence, Smith – though open to criticism of his seamanship – was exonerated of blame and certainly the stories of the bravery he displayed after the collision played a great part in his freedom from guilt in the eyes of the inquirers. From the very onset of the news of the disaster, the fate of this formerly admired and trusted seaman was a subject to grab the journalists' attention and over a period of time, several versions of his fate appeared, which can be listed as follows:

1. The Suicide. One of the first reports about Smith's death was that he had committed suicide by shooting himself. This was first reported by the Reuters news agency in a telegram printed in the "Daily Mirror" and there was also a later statement given by a man named Googht, from Philadelphia, though there had been nobody of that name aboard the Titanic. The latter claimed that Smith and the chief engineer had shot themselves (so too ran other reports about First Officer Murdoch and possibly Chief Officer Wilde and/or Purser McElroy). The Googht report claimed that when Smith's intent was clear, the bridge crew had struggled to wrest the gun from him, but Smith had broken away from the bridge and shot himself through the mouth.

There was also a report from a Dr. J. F. Kemp, a passenger on the Carpathia, who had spoken to a boy from the Titanic who purported to have been one of the last to leave her. According to Dr. Kemp, the boy had said, 'Captain Smith put a pistol to his head and then fell down.'

2. The Return To The Bridge. Steward Edward Brown stated that not long before the Titanic sank, he saw Smith, still clutching his megaphone, walk onto the bridge to wait for the end. Trimmer Samuel Hemmings, however, did not see the captain there when he wandered onto the bridge at about the same time. Harold Bride, who had been one of the last people to talk to Smith, said he was himself in the water when, looking back at the sinking Titanic, he saw Smith jump into the sea from one of the wings of the bridge. George A. Boden claimed that he had last seen Smith being knocked over by the sea water as he struggled to keep a foothold on the slanting deck, whilst G.A. Drayton said that Smith had been swept off the bridge when it lunged forward: 'I saw him swim back onto the sinking ship,' Drayton said. 'He went down with it in my sight.'

3. The Rescuer. Both fireman Harry Senior and Charles Williams, a racquet coach from Harrow School, said that they had seen Smith in the water after the ship had sunk. Both of them told approximately the same story, that Smith swam up to one of the

lifeboats clutching a small child under one arm, whom he handed into the boat. Williams claimed that Smith had gasped, 'Take the child,' before asking, 'What became of Murdoch?' Upon being told that the first officer was surely dead, the captain refused to be rescued and either swam away or let himself sink beneath the waves.

4. <u>Following The Ship.</u> Seaman G.A. Hogg said, 'I saw Captain Smith in the water alongside a raft. "There's the skipper," I yelled, "Give him a hand." They did but he shook himself free and shouted "Good-bye boys, I'm going to follow the ship." That was the last we saw of our skipper.'

A swimmer hailed the boat containing Walter Hurst and kept cheering 'Good boy; good lads!' The voice struck Hurst as belonging to a man who was used to being in a position of authority. Hurst held out an oar to the man, but he was too far gone and when the oar touched him it was clear that the man was dead in the water. For the rest of his life, Hurst was convinced that the man had been Smith.

Seaman McGough claimed that he saw Smith in the water and heard him call to the boat, 'Don't mind me, men; God bless you.' Then he vanished under the water.

There was also an early tale that one of the cooks had seen Smith in the water and sought to pull him aboard a lifeboat, but Smith had pulled away, saying 'Let me go.'

5. <u>Being British.</u> Smith's most famous statement: 'Be British!' or 'Be British, my lads, be British!', which he supposedly yelled through his megaphone to the passengers and crew during the ship's last desperate moments, does not seem to have any basis in fact. Indeed, the story is ridiculous as Smith was well aware that many of his passengers and some of his crew were not British nor even European. Attempts to track down the source of this legend show that it is clear that none of the survivors from the Titanic ever publicly claimed that 'Be British' were the captain's last words. On the other hand, it is not easy to find any other origin for the saying, though it has been suggested that it was attributed to him by a naval officer during one of the earliest memorial services for the victims of the Titanic, possibly the service held at St. Paul's Cathedral on 19th

April 1912. The earliest that the phrase was quoted in the "Staffordshire Sentinel" was in a report of a memorial service held at St. Mark's Church, Shelton, on 5th May of that year.

In pre-World War One Britain, which was still effectively Victorian in its ways of thinking, the phrase seems to have gained instant popularity due to its jingoistic and patriotic nature. Many people seemed to feel that it was the sort of thing 'he would have said', which seems to imply that even the most ardent advocate of the 'Be British' statement was not entirely convinced of its authenticity. Smith's real last order appears to have been the far more prosaic, 'Every man for himself.'

6. "Whispering" Smith. Despite the freezing sea temperatures that killed everyone left in the water, there were some suggestions that Smith may have survived and had somehow managed to reach America undetected. A week after the disaster, a fellow sea captain who claimed to have been acquainted with Smith said that he had seen him alive and well in Baltimore. Several years later, a down-and-out in Ohio, who was known locally as "Whispering" Smith, claimed shortly before his death that he was the former captain of the Titanic!

It is now generally accepted by historians of the Titanic that the most likely of these fates (i.e. the best documented) was that Smith returned to the bridge to await his fate. Certainly it could have been as Harold Bride or G.A. Drayton claimed that Smith either dived or was swept off the bridge when the Titanic plunged. If that was the case it was also possible that Smith could have swum around in the water for a time and may have rescued a child or refused to let himself be rescued, but it has been argued that this could not have happened because his body was never found. However, the human body is not in itself naturally buoyant and once the lungs are inundated with water it will sink. The only bodies found were those of people who had gone into the sea wearing life preservers; the rest sank and Smith was never seen wearing a life preserver.

The suicide story is unlikely. The Reuters report was soon identified as a mistake, a mix-up of two separate messages, nor were there any witnesses other than the unidentified Googht and the child seen by Dr. Kemp, which there would have been had things happened as stated. A precedent that may apply in this case is the verified story that took place about six years before the Titanic disaster of a German sea captain who caused something of a scandal when, after accidentally beaching his ship, he shot himself. It may be that journalists and witnesses had got crossed wires between the two stories.

"Be British!", the best known but least likely of endings, can perhaps be safely put down to sheer sensationalism. The appearances of Smith in America can be attributed to a case of mistaken identity and the ramblings of a worn-out old man seeking a morsel of fame, which perhaps he has gained. All said though, the only certain thing about Smith's fate was that he was dead – the captain had gone down with his ship. Considering the odium heaped upon Ismay, Lord Duff Gordon and Captain Lord, it was probably just as well that Smith had died, as had he lived the scandal would probably have destroyed him.

The effect on Smith's family, as with all of those whose loved ones had died, was terrible. Eleanor Smith was shattered by the news and her one consolation was that she had been one of the first to know that her husband was dead; she did not have the days of agony waiting outside the White Star offices in Southampton, where every morning hundreds of people gathered to read the list of survivors' names. Newspapers reporting the scenes were surprised to see the upper classes mingling in with the crowd of sea-wives and labourers. The disaster cut a swathe across the class system of pre-First World War Britain like nothing previously seen, though in years to follow, this intermingling became a common spectacle. Outside the White Star offices were posted dozens of notices, one of which was a small, sad message from the captain's widow:

'To my fellow sufferers,
My heart overflows with grief for you all and is laden with the sorrow that you are weighed down with, and with this terrible burden that has been thrust upon us. May God be with us and comfort us all. Yours in deep sympathy
ELEANOR SMITH.'

The country was plunged into a wave of mourning and in virtually every church memorial services were held, prayers said for the dead and thanks given for the living. One of the earliest memorial services was held in Southampton and was attended by Eleanor. The greatest service took place on 19th April at St. Paul's Cathedral, where Sir Christopher Wren's masterpiece was packed to overflowing. Dozens of memorial postcards were published, some to raise funds for the families of the dead and there were many that needed such support. In Southampton, from where the Titanic had drawn most of her crew, whole streets saw their menfolk decimated and no money coming in for the foreseeable future. The Titanic's band had its own special fund as there was no provision for the families of the dead men because the band was not officially a part of the crew, but travelled as second-class passengers. Concerts were held, collections made, scores of pieces of bad poetry written to commemorate the disaster and insipid sentimental sheet music such as "My Sweetheart Went Down With The Ship" was churned out. Friends even handed one another mourning cards in commemoration of the Titanic and her dead.

However, when what had started as genuine grief and sorrow for the victims and their families began to turn into something more rabid, somebody had to speak up. One of the leading literary lights of the day, playwright George Bernard Shaw, in a fit of pique wrote a letter to the "Daily News and Leader" on 14th May 1912, in which he basically said that he was being driven to distraction by the romantic image being painted around the disaster. Smith came in for some special treatment within the confines of his arguments, as Shaw was contemptuous of the captain being presented as some sort of super-hero towering over a shipload of other "British" heroes. Six days later, Sir Arthur Conan Doyle wrote a reply in which he virtually accused Shaw of lying and of showing a complete lack of compassion. Shaw attacked again on 22nd May, saying that if anyone was sentimental or foolish enough to remind him that Smith had gone down with his ship, they should be reminded that so too had the ship's cat!

Though many of the examples that Shaw touched upon in his arguments (including the story of Smith shooting himself) have since been dismissed as unlikely, he did have a number of good points to make. By this time a lot of pretty awful patriotic nonsense was being attached to Smith's name, some of it dangerous nonsense as it distorted facts and attempted to cover up mistakes. Shaw was trying to shake sense into people and make them see that what had happened was a disaster of unparalleled dimensions, the lessons of which had been learnt the hard way because of mistakes in law, in operational procedures and in command; the disaster was not an exercise designed to prove the nobility of the British in adversity. Conan Doyle for the conservative view, however, did not like Shaw's radical tone. Conan Doyle's thoughts were with the victims of the disaster and their families, one of which was the Smith family to whom Shaw's comments would have read as nothing short of boorish insensitivity at such a time.

Shaw's views were, however, the exception rather than the rule. During the inquiries into the disaster, few aspersions had been cast on the captain's character. Men such as Herbert Lightoller, the most senior of the Titanic's surviving officers, were fully prepared to defend their former captain to the hilt. To many, notably the rich passengers who had been cultivated by Smith as a group of friends and valued customers, such a defence seemed perfectly correct and there was a general will amongst them to say nothing but good about the dead. The tales of Smith's last moments spurred them on, notably the stories of him rescuing a child and his super-patriotic "last order", 'Be British!', both of which appealed powerfully to their sensibilities. To them such nobility of spirit surely demanded a permanent memorial. The obvious place to put this would be in the town of his birth.

However, this idea did not receive a great deal of support in the Potteries, where the name Edward John Smith was hardly known beyond the circle of his old friends or those who remembered him in connection with the grocer's in Well Street. The local newspaper, the "Staffordshire Sentinel", had quickly latched onto his connection with the Potteries and naturally followed the stories of his fate with interest and, to the paper's credit, with little sensationalism. Despite this, few people wished to be associated with the greatest maritime disaster in history, for fear perhaps that the curse of the Titanic might be catching. The controversy was, therefore, felt very powerfully in what in 1910 had become the Federation of Stoke-on-Trent. For this group of towns aspiring towards city status, the news of Smith's connection with the area was not seen as a good advertisement. No-one denied that Smith had died bravely, but, as the local historian W.M. Jamieson implied, Smith had embarrassed the Potteries. So far as most of the federal council could see, Smith had not done anything for the area other than forever associate it with the Titanic disaster. Because of this the council pretended that the man had never existed and there was no move to commemorate Smith's death officially.

Though there was to be no official recognition of Smith, many of his old friends felt that they should make an effort to maintain his memory in his home town. William M. Hampton, an old friend, backed by many of the Etruria British School's old boys, immediately proposed to start a subscription list for a memorial tablet. Hardly two days had passed since the disaster when, on 17th April, the "Staffordshire Sentinel" carried this appeal, under the title 'Proposed Hanley Memorial to Captain Smith':

'Sir – Might I suggest it would be a gracious act to place a memorial tablet in some public building in Hanley to the memory of the late Captain E.J. Smith of the Titanic?

It is well known that he was a native of Hanley, and I have (amongst many others who are now with us) known him personally since his schooldays, and have watched his career and have been proud that Hanley has produced such an eminent seaman. There are no doubt many who would like to show respect to his memory by subscribing towards the memorial. I would like to name 2s. 6d. as the limit of the subscriptions.

Would it be asking too much for your sympathy in the matter, and receive any subscriptions which may be sent.

         – Yours etc.   W.M. Hampton. Eastwood and Mousecroft Fire Brick and Marl Works, Hanley, April 17th 1912.'

Subscriptions began to arrive, but they didn't exactly flood in and a short time afterwards another letter appeared in the "Sentinel", this time from Mr. Hampton's son, Thomas, who tried to jolt the local lethargy with a dose of patriotism:

'... I am sure there are hundreds of people in the Potteries who would only be too pleased to subscribe to such a fund to show our appreciation of Captain Smith's gallant conduct in this terrible disaster.

Not only are "we Potters" proud that he was an Englishman, but that he was a Potteryman and a Briton to the backbone.'

But this didn't work either. Subscriptions still only trickled in and it seems that the Hamptons were probably tapping the wrong vein at the wrong time with this overt plea to sentiment. It was made at the same time as many national newspapers were reporting several of the less favourable rumours concerning Smith's fate, notably the story of him shooting himself in despair.

Eventually, though, enough contributions were taken and a total of £21 0s. 6d. was raised. Shortly before the ceremony, which took place a year and a day after the disaster, a list naming the 90-odd contributors was printed in the "Staffordshire Sentinel". It had been decided that the plaque to Captain Smith was to be placed in the entrance to Hanley Town Hall and so it was that at 3 p.m. on Tuesday 16th April 1913, the mayor stood up before a large crowd of dignitaries and officially unveiled the Potteries' only memorial to the captain of the Titanic, an ornamental cast metal plaque which read:

'THIS TABLET IS DEDICATED TO THE MEMORY OF COM-MANDER EDWARD JOHN SMITH, R.D., R.N.R. BORN IN HANLEY, 27th JANY 1850, DIED AT SEA, 15th APRIL 1912.

BE BRITISH.

WHILST IN COMMAND OF THE WHITE STAR S.S. "TITANIC" THAT GREAT SHIP STRUCK AN ICEBERG IN THE ATLANTIC OCEAN DURING THE NIGHT AND SPEEDILY SANK WITH NEARLY ALL WHO WERE ON BOARD. CAPTAIN SMITH HAVING DONE ALL MAN COULD DO FOR THE SAFETY OF PASSENGERS AND CREW REMAINED AT HIS POST ON THE SINKING SHIP UNTIL THE END. HIS LAST MESSAGE TO HIS CREW WAS "BE BRITISH".'

A GALLANT NAME

The memorial tablet remained there until 1961, when during alterations to the town hall it was decided that there was no more room for it and it was handed over to Smith's old school, or rather the school that had replaced it. The British School had long since disappeared and had been replaced in 1881 by a larger, brick-built, Gothic-style board school, which still exists today, though it ceased to operate as a school in 1978.

Back in 1913, though, on 22nd April, a week after the ceremony in Hanley, a similar event took place at the board school – this time to unveil a portrait. It was a photograph of Smith dressed in his white uniform and was presented to the school by some of its old boys, with the proviso that the ornately framed photograph was to be fixed in a conspicuous place in the school. The portrait hung there for many years and was later joined by the plaque from Hanley Town Hall. Before the school closed, the photograph was copied by "Sentinel" photographer and local historian, E.J.D. Warrillow, and now forms a part of the extensive Warrillow collection of photographs held at Keele University.

Before the ceremony took place, some of the old boys who had known Smith in his youth were asked to write to Eleanor Smith. It was a good plan and their recollections form the basis of the first chapter of this book, but it must have been a duty tinged with sadness for all concerned. Spencer Till and Edmund Jones wrote from the Potteries, while Joe Turner, by then the manager of Nobell's explosives factory, wrote from Perranporth in Cornwall. Eleanor replied to their letters with some passion, telling them that her husband had often joyfully recalled his childhood. However, Eleanor did not attend the unveiling ceremony, but Spencer Till spoke in her stead, relating to those gathered at the board school that he had recently had occasion to meet Eleanor when she paid a visit to a lifelong friend in Runcorn. During the visit, Mrs. Smith had shown Till a number of photographs of her husband, one being of him attending a large banquet thrown in his honour at the so-called "Millionaires' Club" in New York. The Americans referred to Captain Smith as 'The old man of the sea', Eleanor had informed him, and his popularity with wealthy and famous Americans was unassailable, as Till had recognised many eminent men in the photograph.

Somewhat irked by the lack of enthusiasm in the Potteries, in November 1913, the eminent men and women of Britain and America banded together in support of the Captain Smith Memorial Committee, which had been set up in Britain by a number of influential friends of the Titanic's skipper, notably the Bishop of Willesden, Lady Astor and the Duchess of Sutherland. The committee's brief was to provide what they deemed a more fitting memorial to the old sailor. They had their hearts set on a statue, but there was also to be a stained glass window for Liverpool Cathedral and any extra money was to be donated to the Seaman's Orphanage in Southampton. Subscriptions to the fund were plentiful from the well-heeled citizens of Britain and America, but the committee received only three contributions from the Potteries.

The sculptress chosen for the commission of Smith's statue was Lady Kathleen Scott, the widow of Captain Robert Falcon Scott, "Scott of the Antarctic", whose expedition to the South Pole in 1912 had ended so tragically for him and his men. The coming together of these two figures, Smith and Scott, both of them ripe for deification by the Establishment, is interesting to compare and contrast. Lady Scott, perhaps still in mourning, nonetheless got down to work and soon decided upon constructing a bronze statue 7 feet 8 inches high, to be mounted on a 7 feet high pedestal of Cornish granite. The only thing left to do then was to find somewhere to put the statue. The Potteries was approached, but it considered that it had got enough memorials to the man. So the committee were stuck until they lighted upon a small piece of pleasant parkland, nowadays known as Beacon Park, next to the museum in the picturesque south Staffordshire city of Lichfield. The council were approached and, given the county connection with Smith, were willing to think it over. So the park was provisionally cited as the spot for the statue when a fresh controversy broke.

Why had Lichfield been chosen? This was the angry question asked by many of the city's inhabitants when they learned about the statue and a number of them banded together and presented a petition in protest. Their argument was plain and simple – that Smith not only had nothing to do with Lichfield, but was not an historically notable figure. The lame excuses put forward by the memorial committee did not appease them and if anything, only went to show the embarrassment that the committee were beginning to feel about the whole affair. The most artificial excuse offered was that Lichfield lay midway between London and Liverpool and was, therefore, easily accessible to American visitors! However, Lichfield was the capital of the diocese that covered Hanley and had the double advantage of also being in Staffordshire, Smith's native county. The committee then meekly added that they had 'other reasons'. Lichfield was fully aware of these 'other reasons' and the protesters made the perfectly valid statement to the effect that if Hanley did not want this honour, why should Lichfield?

The argument finally came to a head in a well-attended meeting of the Lichfield council. The mayor, Councillor Bridgeman J.P., received the petition of protest only a few weeks before the statue was due to be unveiled in the museum grounds. The mayor said that he wished the whole affair to be discussed before an entire council in committee. However, Councillor Longstaff opposed this move in deference to the petitioners, saying that as it was a public petition, the whole matter should be discussed in open council, to which a group of fellow councillors shouted 'Hear! Hear!' Councillor Longstaff failed to see any reason for taking up the matter in committee. However, Bridgeman opposed the move to an open council, which would delay matters.

'The time is too limited,' he said.

'Why?' asked Councillor Longstaff.

'Because the date is fixed for the unveiling,' answered Bridgeman.

'We have already decided on the job,' added Councillor Jones, supporting the mayor. 'It's too late now.'

Events in the council chamber ebbed and flowed along these lines for a short time, but eventually, the town clerk was called upon to read out the petition from the protesters, which ran thus:

A GALLANT NAME

'June 1914.

To His Worship the Mayor of Lichfield –

With respect to the acceptance of a statue to the late Captain Smith of the "Titanic", and the decision to place the same in the Museum Grounds, we, the undersigned, desire to place before you our reasons for regarding such an action as undesirable, at the same time emphasising the fact that we do not in the least suggest any sense of reproach upon the memory of an admittedly brave sailor:-

i)   His birthplace being in North Staffordshire, there is no claim upon the City.

ii) We are anxious for the reputation of our City that only such monuments should be erected as are by general consensus of opinion, representative of distinctly eminent men.

iii) We do not consider that there is any particular historical reason warranting the perpetuation of Captain Smith's memory in so marked a way as the erection of a statue would signify.

We trust, therefore, that the acceptance of the statue for erection here is not too late for reconsideration, and we respectfully ask that you will bring the matter forward in the right quarter.

In conclusion, we would urge the need for most careful consideration of any claim which purposes so near an association with the one statue of which we are all so justly proud, that of one of our greatest statesmen, the late King Edward VII.'

There followed a list of the 73 petitioners, mostly citizens of Lichfield and a few army officers, the name of each being read out loud by the town clerk. It was pretty clear that more than anything else, the petitioners were rather alienated by the feeling that they were having a rich man's statue foisted onto their city. However, Councillor Raby for the conservatives read out next the names of the contributors to the memorial committee. These included the late Duke of Sutherland, the dowager Duchess of Arran, a former ambassador to the United States, assorted generals, colonels and admirals, churchmen, academics, Members of Parliament, naval captains, merchant commanders and the American writer Kate Douglas, who had apparently written 'a moving tribute' to be read

146

out when the statue was unveiled.

Councillor Raby then added a barb to his argument, by saying that he would have liked to have talked to all who had signed the petition, whom he believed had signed it unthinkingly, and that to him, the petition constituted a 'particularly ungracious' statement. Further warming to his task, Raby drew upon newspaper accounts of Smith's bravery; he mentioned amongst other things that Lady Scott had sculpted the statue and he perpetuated a myth by saying that 'Be British' were 'words that would live as long as the English language'. Councillor Longstaff for the petitioners was, however, still rather doubtful and added that though he felt that the words of the petition were rather unfortunate, he did not see any reason for anyone to launch into a defence of Captain Smith.

Councillor Raby completed his argument by telling the council that Queen Alexandra had been informed of the unveiling ceremony due to take place. That seemed to end the last of the many arguments between the critics and supporters of Smith, with the upshot of it all being that the petition was ordered to lie on the table. The statue was finally accepted because the councillors of Lichfield realised that it had nowhere else to go.

The statue was unveiled on the warm and sunny afternoon of Wednesday 29th July 1914, by Smith's daughter, Helen. The ceremony was attended by all the pomp that could be mustered and a large crowd of onlookers gathered at the museum grounds. On one side of the statue, a large contingent of the Royal Naval Reserve from Liverpool, dressed in their blue jackets, was drawn up under the command of Lieutenant Trant, who was also the White Star Line representative. Also there was a group of army buglers from nearby Whittington Barracks, their splendid scarlet tunics contrasting brilliantly with the blue of the R.N.R. and the green lawn. There were also representatives of the merchant navy, the Royal Navy, the police and the army. Some, however, had been unable to make the ceremony, the largest of these groups being a detachment of the South Staffordshire Regiment, who were to have provided a guard of honour. Instead, they were away on manoeuvres, pending mobilisation, getting ready for the holocaust that was about to engulf half of Europe.

As the civic procession made its way to the platform, the "General Salute" was sounded by the buglers. The procession was headed by the sword and mace bearers, dressed in traditional 'quaint' uniforms, as one reporter put it. Then came the mayor and the sheriff dressed in splendid robes of scarlet and blue. Aldermen and councillors then filed onto the platform, followed by the Bishop of Willesden; the Duchess of Sutherland; the statue's sculptor, Lady Kathleen Scott; Eleanor and Helen Smith; Lord Charles Beresford M.P., dressed in a naval uniform, and F.S. Stevenson, the honorary secretary to the memorial committee. The Mayor of Lichfield presided over the ceremony.

The message from Queen Alexandra was obviously a good starting point and was read out to the crowd:

'Her Majesty, as you are well aware, feels the most sincere and sympathetic interest in this movement and thinks this tribute to the good and brave man who died in the performance of his duties a most appropriate one.'

This perhaps was read out by the Bishop of Willesden; certainly he took over when the Queen's message had passed and he described the three or four journeys he had made with Smith and recalled something of their friendship.

The next to take the platform was the statuesque, elegant and eloquent Duchess of Sutherland, a character well-known to the manufacturers in the Potteries as "Meddlesome Millie", because of her investigation and criticism of the dangerous working practices workers had to endure. Being acquainted with the people of Hanley, she was perhaps the most sympathetic of all to Smith's memory, being able to appreciate the leap he had made since his childhood. When she spoke she drew an instant comparison of Captain Smith with Captain Scott and an aside to Lady Scott accompanied this, as the explorer's widow was an obvious link. The duchess then continued:

'Don't my friends, grieve too much because Captain Smith lies in the sea – the sea that has swallowed silently and fearfully many of the great and many of those we love. Let us take great heart in this most solemn scene to raise our own powers of courage and self-sacrifice so that we may never be lacking in the supreme hour.'

A GALLANT NAME

It was a little flowery for some tastes, perhaps, but against the backcloth of impending war, the duchess was speaking from the heart and the audience appreciated it.

Helen Melville Smith, dressed in a pale hat and dress, sat with her mother near to the statue, quietly listening to these speeches. Eventually, though, she was invited to take the stand and, tugging at the sheeting, she revealed Lady Scott's statue of the captain of the Titanic. To those in the audience who had persevered in the face of criticism and difficulty to get the statue raised, it was a triumph.

Lord Charles Beresford then took the stand and talked about Smith's career, his patriotism and self-sacrifice, as too in various ways did the many others who got up in turn to speak: the Marquess of Salisbury; publisher J.G. Hodder-Williams of Hodder & Stoughton; Lady Diana Manners, a brilliant society figure, and her sister, the Marchioness of Anglesey.

This all went on for some time, but when the ceremony ended it was with a vote of thanks being extended to Lady Scott and to Helen Smith. Eleanor Smith ended the ceremony by placing at the foot of the statue a wreath of red and white roses in memory of her husband.

It had been a proud day for those relations of Edward John Smith who had lived to see this moment, but with it, the family faded from the limelight. Eleanor remained a widow, though she lived to see her only child married, with Helen later becoming Mrs. Simon Russell Cooke. Eleanor met a tragic end, when she was killed in a road accident on 28th April 1931. Helen died in 1972.

There were also the Hancock and Harrington families who could feel pride in their most famous relative and many of them attended the unveiling ceremony. Thirza Harrington, at 78 the grand matriarch of the Smith and Hancock clan since the deaths of Edward and Catherine Smith, was there with many of her children and grandchildren; so too was James William Sidney Harrington, who had served under Smith aboard the Lizzie Fennell, and with him were his wife and children. Today, there are still descendants of these two families who can look back fondly to the day before World War One, when the wealthy of the old and new worlds gathered in Lichfield to raise a statue to a potter's son from Hanley.

The statue is still there, as described in the prologue. How popular it has been in the intervening years is open to debate – we will never know how many visiting Americans have stopped off at Lichfield. What is known, though , is that Captain Smith never gained cult status as a popular hero as did Captain Scott. To his old friends it must have seemed that the infamy of the ship had destroyed the man. But in the long run the Titanic was also his saviour, for as Captain Smith the superhero was rapidly forgotten, the story of the Titanic passed into popular legend and has proved to be the most enduring of his memorials.

9

The Durable Legend

Several days after the statue of Captain Smith was unveiled in Lichfield, World War One broke out and as it created even greater horrors and grief, memories of the Titanic disaster seemed to fade. Yet even after two world wars, the mystique surrounding this great ship, the cameos of bravery, self-sacrifice and luck recounted by survivors, the controversy the disaster aroused and its powerful sense of tragedy have ensured that rather than fading, the story has gained the status of popular myth – the 'unsinkable' Titanic, the last great Victorian folly. Forever in the public imagination are her glancing blow with an iceberg, with the sea as calm as a mill pond; the 'splendid discipline'; the band playing "Nearer My God To Thee"; the Californian incident; 'women and children first' and the captain's last order, 'Be British'. All of these are elements, some true, some false, of a tale familiar to millions – a warning to man not to be so confident of his control over the forces of nature.

Modern interest in the Titanic began during the 1950s as the memories of war faded and people began to look back to the peaceful days, before World War One shattered their illusions of safety. Perhaps it was this pessimistic view that things are never as safe as they appear that attracted so many people to the story of the Titanic. Also, the tale of the Titanic seemed almost Greek or Shakespearean in its tragic grandeur, containing as it did the inevitable irony of the 'unsinkable' ship sinking so helplessly on its first outing. It seems with hindsight to contain a wry comment on all of those optimistic thoughts of the early twentieth century; the 'unsinkable' ship sank and the war that followed it, the war they said would be over by Christmas, the war 'to end all wars', lasted for four bloody years, before spilling over into further conflict in the 1930s.

In the four decades since this resurgence of interest in the

Titanic, hundreds, perhaps thousands, of books and articles have been written or rescued from obscurity. The early British and American inquiry reports have been republished, as too have survivors' accounts of the disaster. There have been technical reports and histories of shipping and shipwrecks. Other works have concentrated on the story, the ship and her people. A few have dealt with related subjects, such as the Californian incident, Thomas Andrews and shipbuilding and Marconi and his wireless system. There have also been books that dealt with the psychic forewarnings of disaster.

Of the early books written there are perhaps only a handful that are useful to any modern study of the Titanic, the most notable of these being Sir Phillip Gibbs' "The Deathless Story of the Titanic", published originally in 1912, but still in wide circulation as a reprint. Unlike many contemporary accounts, it usually steers clear of the flights of fancy of the time and is very useful in that it is not only well illustrated, but also contains lists of passengers and crew, stating who was lost and saved. But after the initial ballyhoo was over, though the Titanic was still the stuff of legend, there were no authoritative accounts of the disaster until Walter Lord's "A Night to Remember", which was published in 1955 after twenty years of research on his part. Told from dozens of personal viewpoints and with statements drawn from the official inquiries into the disaster, it is still generally regarded as the best rendition of the story, though it has been widely criticised by the supporters of Captain Stanley Lord.

Many modern books on the Titanic (and there are a great many) concentrate more on the peripheral details about the ship and her people. It is not surprising to find that some of the best books in this respect are products of members of the Titanic Historical Society in the U.S.A., a society originally set up in 1963 under the rather odd sounding title, "Titanic Enthusiasts of America". Since its foundation, the society has not only gone on to produce some excellent books, but also acts as a great repository of information on the ship, its two sisters and the White Star Line in general. The society has a collection of artefacts from the ship housed at the Philadelphia Marine Museum.

In the wake of the disaster there was also a wave of songs written about the Titanic – over 300 in all. Almost immediately, as the news of the disaster was coming in, about four separate pieces of sheet music were produced, such as "The Wreck of the Titanic" and the overly sentimental "My Sweetheart Went Down With The Ship". However, most of these songs died a death (some might say thankfully) and only a few are still sung. A couple of them were released as gramophone records as well as music for the piano and though they are not perhaps worth much in themselves, because of their connection with the disaster they are now a part of a range of Titanic collectables for a growing number of enthusiasts.

For these, the most precious items, of course, are objects that came from the Titanic herself, but such objects are now almost entirely the province of the rich collector or museums with large budgets. An example of how much a genuine Titanic article can fetch was demonstrated by the auction in London on 13th April 1992 – almost 80 years to the day of the disaster – of a series of wireless messages sent from the liner that fetched a staggering £95,700! Cards posted from the ship that bear either the Cherbourg or Queenstown postmark are also extremely rare and of greatly increasing value. Some of these have gone to collectors, but there are doubtless still many held by the families or descendants of those whose loved ones died in the disaster, for whom the sentimental value of such objects outweighs their monetary worth.

However, cards of the Titanic, or related to the Titanic, are more reasonably priced, but as the desire for such items has increased, so too has their scarcity and value. Before the disaster the White Star Line produced a series of "company cards" that could be posted from their own ships – they were a cheap and easy form of publicity and served relatively the same functions as any modern seaside postcard. Following in the wake of the disaster, though, there was an explosion in the market as dozens of types of memorial postcards were produced. These often carried just pictures of the Titanic (or the Olympic or even Cunard's Mauretania disguised as the Titanic). Often, though, these pictures were augmented with painted-on icebergs or accompanied by pictures of well-known passengers and crew, with a perennial favourite being Captain Smith. Many were of a sentimental or religious nature, but many were produced in response to the sort of "Dunkirk spirit" that the disaster was promoted as epitomizing.

Today there is still a range of Titanic-related collectables for those who cannot afford even the cheapest of the old cards. Many of the cards have been reprinted and can be found occasionally, but the most readily accessible items are plastic models of the Titanic. There are clocks with Titanic motifs, towels with the ship's name printed on them, Titanics in a bottle and seaside key rings of the captain's cabin, S.S. Titanic. For those in the Potteries who like their collectables in liquid form, there is now a brewery in the city named after the ship and it not only produces some fine beers, but also has Titanic beer mats. Captain Smith also received further immortality in a range of miniature statuettes produced for the 80th anniversary of the disaster.

Perhaps the main reason why the Titanic disaster is still so alive in the public imagination is the fact that it is such a dramatic story, which has lent itself not only to many books, but also to several films. If the broadsheets, memorial postcards and booklets of the early twentieth century created the first popular images of the disaster, then in our own age it is the medium of the film that has gone the furthest in spreading the story.

As early as 1929, a movie based on the disaster was in production. Based on a play entitled "The Berg" by Ernest Raymond, the film and the ship in the story were called "Atlantic", though the tale was framed loosely around that of the Titanic. Made by British International Pictures, directed by E.A. Dupont and shot by the American, Charles Rosher, "Atlantic" was classified as a 'spectacular'. More than that it was a "talkie" – Dupont's first, starring John Longdon and Madeleine Carroll at the head of a large cast. According to critics, though, it was a wasted effort, as what could have been a powerful film was ruined by banal dialogue, wooden acting, boring photography and an all too obvious use of models. One critic (writing in the 1950s) also noted that the water levels kept going up and down. Simultaneous with the English version, a German edition of the same story was shot on the same sound stages.

It was in Germany that the second cinematic version of the tale of the Titanic was produced, albeit in a twisted manner, when Dr. Goebbels' state propaganda machine produced a Nazi version of the story in the film "Titanic". This was designed as the principal anti-British film of 1942 and was released in 1943. It was directed by Herbert Selpin and Werner Klinger. In the film, the villain was represented as J. Bruce Ismay who caused the disaster through a blind desire to win the blue riband, regardless of the risks to passengers and crew. Smith was represented as an acolyte in this vainglorious attempt. It perhaps comes as no surprise to find that the hero of the story was a square-jawed German ship's officer, who did his best to prove Ismay's guilt, though he failed in his attempt! The story was twisted beyond belief and apparently humorously so, with the German officer and his wife being magnificently calm while everybody else was panicking. The storyline was also violently anti-Jewish, the motive behind the attempt for the blue riband being supposedly some sort of Jewish plot, so it may go as read that no mention was made of the bravery and dignity with which the Jewish Straus's met their end. In the event, the film was not successful, Selpin committed suicide, which Nazi directors had a habit of doing, and its initial release in Germany was cancelled as it was feared that the scenes of panic might remind people of the terror caused by the R.A.F.'s bombing of Germany's big cities. The film was eventually released in occupied Paris in 1943.

The first truly big screen treatment, though, was naturally from Hollywood, in the 1953 movie, "Titanic", which was a visually impressive production, especially in the scenes depicting the ship's mid-Atlantic collision with the iceberg. The cast was a strong one, headed by solid Clifton Webb and the ever-sultry Barbara Stanwyck as Mr. and Mrs. Sturges. Stanwyck played a wilful wife and mother, who was taking her children to America to grow up as 'normal people', far from the claustrophobic old world life style of her husband. The film's greatest weakness was that it concentrated on fictional characters, whose rather humdrum adventures paled beside the real dramas of that night. Nor did a rather melodramatic script, with such lines as, 'We might be having sand for supper,' really do the film a service! The crew, though, were depicted fairly faithfully and the actor Brian Aherne gave a strong performance of grace under pressure as Captain Smith. For content the movie was something of a non-starter, but it was a spectacular film nevertheless and one that has only recently been superseded. Not only did this come across on the screen, but even the actors on the spot were overcome by the magnitude of what they were involved in. During production at the 20th Century Fox water tank, seated in a lifeboat hanging 47 feet up the side of a mock-up of the Titanic, Miss Stanwyck gained a sort of empathy with the people who had actually had to go through this in reality and when, as the boat was being lowered, she caught a glance up at those left behind to "die" with the ship, she burst into a flood of uncontrollable tears. She said everything had suddenly seemed so real.

Her sentiments were no doubt echoed by many watching the finest film ever made about the disaster, the painstaking and often highly moving British film, "A Night to Remember" (1958), based on Walter Lord's factual best-seller. A number of years ago in an interview for a children's education programme about the Titanic disaster, one of its survivors, Eva Hart, remarked that this was the one film she could not fault and the critics have almost unanimously agreed. Though it was not a great box office success at the time, the film, released by the Rank organisation, is today widely regarded as one of those rare birds, a classic, post-war British film, and as such was one in a series of videos released several years ago. Produced by William MacQuitty, who as a boy had seen the Titanic launched, the film was produced on what by modern standards was a shoestring budget – £499,670. If the film had a fault, it was that it did lack a little in special effects and some of the model shots were a bit obvious. But the script carried the story, mostly because the screenplay, which was written with some flair by novelist Eric Ambler, stuck to reported dialogue or a near approximation. The film starred Kenneth More as Second Officer Lightoller, but it was full of many beautifully acted roles. Lawrence Naismyth landed the part of Smith and, though a little shorter than the man himself, he shined in his pivotal role, breathing great life into the character, first as the genial host, then as the concerned captain and finally as the resigned tragic hero. His last scenes were rather moving as he bawled out, 'Abandon ship! Every man for himself!' through his megaphone, before he walked back onto the bridge to await his fate.

After this, there was a T.V. film, "S.O.S. Titanic", starring the late David Janssen, which, like Hollywood's "Titanic", concentrated on the lives and loves of fictional characters. Then there was a brief scene in Terry Gilliam's fantasy adventure "Time Bandits", where the time-travelling dwarfs and their boy companion were sipping cocktails aboard the ship as the collision occurred.

Television too took to the theme of time travel to explore the seemingly unavoidable fate of the Titanic, for example in the very first episode of the 1960s science fiction series "The Time Tunnel". In this episode, the two time-travellers found themselves aboard the Titanic, where, despite beating up the Marconi men and making an unscheduled CQD call, as well as coming armed with the next day's newspaper, they were unable to convince the captain (played by Michael Rennie) of the impending disaster.

As far as films go, a variation on the theme of the Titanic was not so successful. "Raise the Titanic" in 1980 sank as helplessly as the ship itself. The story of the Titanic having gone down with a valuable element that could be used in late twentieth century weapons production seemed a surefire hit after the successful novel of the same name. But despite a budget of an estimated $40 million, the star feature of which was a meticulously detailed 55-foot scale model of the Titanic, costing $400,000, the film was a flop, returning only $10 million. Lord Grade, who had sponsored the movie, was reported to have commented that it would have been cheaper to have lowered the Atlantic!

The most recent film offering, James Cameron's multi-Oscar-winning epic "Titanic", released in 1997, was yet another fictional rendering of the old story, told this time in flashback from the present day. The main plot revolved around a young couple, Rose De Witt Bukater (Kate Winslet), a pretty, spoilt, but spirited first-class girl, and Jack Dawson (Leonardo DiCaprio), a handsome, but impoverished artist travelling on a steerage ticket. After Jack had stopped Rose from throwing herself overboard, a rather unlikely romance ensued, which was interrupted by the now infamous mid-Atlantic collision. This put their love to the test and our two heroes were forced to endure a series of adventures through the bowels of the doomed liner, finding themselves at last hanging onto the very stern rails where they had first met, just as the Titanic went down. All this took place in the presence of many of the "real-life" passengers and crew, one of whom was Captain Smith, ably played by Bernard Hill, who displayed some of the shock that must have struck the old captain when he realised what had happened. However, rather than the conscientious captain of the history books, Smith was depicted as a rather lack-lustre individual, easily swayed by J. Bruce Ismay into imperiling his ship and doing little to help in the subsequent evacuation.

This, alas, was not the only instance the film offered of the scriptwriters tampering with history. For example, the steerage passengers were kept locked up much longer and much more forcefully than they actually were. Moreover, the collision here was apparently caused by Fred Fleet ogling our two lovers when he should have been looking out for icebergs, and in one melo-dramatic scene First Officer Murdoch was depicted blowing his brains out after gunning down an irate passenger. If that were not strange enough, Jack, our handsome hero from steerage, wandered around first class as if he owned the ship!

However, it was neither historical veracity nor storyline that made this film so memorable. That honour belonged almost solely to the special effects that took the lion's share of the film's estimated $200 million budget. With its massive mock-up of the Titanic, meticulous interior sets and state-of-the-art computer graphics, the latter half of the film was quite stunning to behold. Indeed, never has the demise of the R.M.S. Titanic been so realistically portrayed.

The interest generated by this film, however, was only the latest stage of a renewed fascination with the Titanic disaster that was kindled a decade earlier. It was in 1985 that the remarkable news was flashed around the world that a joint French and American team had discovered the wreck of the ship. She lay 13,000 feet down on the ocean floor, upright, but broken in two, which effectively scuppered any hopes that the Titanic might be raised.

The story of the discovery is in itself a tale of great human endeavour, nowhere better told than in Dr. Ballard's fascinating and beautifully illustrated book, "The Discovery of the Titanic", which on its publication became an international best seller. The team he led aboard the oceanic research vessel, Knorr, was one of scientists, technicians, oceanographers, electricians, sonar experts, skilled ancillary workers drawn from his own Woods Hole Oceanographic Institute in Massachusetts, and a team from the French IFREMER (Institut Français de Recherches pour l'Exploitation des Mers – the French national institute of oceanography) under his co-leader Jean-Louis Michel. Each nation brought to the expedition its own brand of expertise; both the French and the Americans were the leading authorities on deep water exploration, the French with the bathoscope or sonar and the Americans with the submersible.

Dr. Ballard, an ocean geologist by profession, had long considered the problems of exploring the deep places of the world's oceans and admitted himself that at first his desire to search for the Titanic was merely a means to an end, a popular idea to use to attract sponsors for his schemes. The ends he envisioned were massive leaps forward in deep underwater exploration, not only with sonar, but with the visual image via deep tow or tethered robotic cameras. His grandest concept was what he named "Jason", a robot that could explore the ocean floor for man, without the scientist ever leaving the surface. However, Jason was a long way off and in the meantime his desire to find the Titanic became an obsession.

The expedition started in late June 1985; there was a "weather window" until mid-September for operations in the area where the Titanic had sunk and as it turned out they nearly ran out of time. With the help of the French team (aboard their own ship, le Suroit) Dr. Ballard searched for the Titanic with "Argo", a deep-tow camera, a battery of still and video cameras loaded with ultra light-sensitive film, set in a tubular frame, which was "flown" over the seabed on 13,000 feet of cable. Argo was originally conceived as the mother craft to Jason, but for this expedition Argo flew alone.

While the French scanned the seabed with a complex sonar system, Argo flew from Knorr. The days passed into weeks and into months as the ships executed sweeps of a grid. By late August everyone was tired and Ballard even had to ward off what he described as a 'minor mutiny' at about this time. But fortune was to smile on them. In the early hours of 1st September, 'The Watch of Quiet Excellence' was going through the established routine of observing a battery of monitor screens showing images from Argo's cameras, when something flickered into view. Momentary surprise gave way to jubilation as suddenly the crew realised that they were looking at a ship's boiler – a Titanic boiler. No-one wanted to leave the room as they savoured this moment in history and only when the cook popped his head into the cabin did they send him off to find Ballard. Soon everyone aboard was going into the cabin to get a look at the increasing field of wreckage that flashed before Argo's cameras and a party atmosphere took over as the team celebrated on cheap wine.

At 2 a.m., somebody noted that it was near to the time that the Titanic had sunk. Dr. Ballard, who had never lost sight of the human tragedy at the centre of his quest, marked the discovery with a very human gesture. At 2.20, he went out onto the Knorr's fantail deck, where a small crowd then gathered, and a brief memorial service was held for the 1,522 people who had perished during a night 73 years earlier. Overhead, next to the Stars and Stripes, flew the Harland and Wolff flag, raised in honour of the ship having been found.

The discovery was headline news around the world. Knorr returned to Woods Hole to meet with a grand reception – a flotilla of small boats and a huge crowd of well-wishers, spectators and newsmen, all eager to get the first words of this great discovery. But when the euphoria was over, Ballard was determined to return to the Titanic. This he did a year later aboard a second Woods Hole ship, Atlantis II, from which a series of dives was made down to the Titanic in the three-man submersible, Alvin. This time, the expedition brought with it a partial realisation of Ballard's dream, a small prototype robot camera that was operated from a cradle attached to Alvin. The camera was named "Jason Junior" or "J.J." for short.

For the first dive there was only time to locate the Titanic, on account of technical problems. Even so, the crew's first encounter with the ship overwhelmed them. After a two-hour drop in total darkness, Alvin had skied over the seabed, when suddenly it encountered a wall of steel that seemed to reach up forever. On successive dives, the sheer size of the ship was a constant source of amazement for each new crewman. With each dive there was something new and interesting to see and despite a few teething troubles, J.J. gave excellent results. Its most spectacular trip was down into the first-class restaurant, an adventure that caused one of the crew to quip that they had been 'dancing in the ballroom'.

The footage showed clearly that the bow of the ship was the most intact, though its nose was buried in the mud almost to the anchors after it had sunk from the surface. The foremast had collapsed backwards, the bridge had been destroyed and the funnels sheered off, whilst the back half of this part of the wreckage ended with the torn and mangled decks where the ship had broken up. On one occasion, J.J. took a peek at Smith's cabin which was partially collapsed. The window was open and as it operated on a worm screw, this could not have occurred accidentally, so Ballard mused that perhaps Smith had decided to let a little air into his cabin on that fateful night in 1912. There was a debris field beyond the wreck of the bow and, amid the scattered boilers, sections of plate steel and the contents that had spilled out of the ship when she broke up, lay the wrecked stern of the Titanic. This was far more damaged than the bow, having pancaked as it hit the ocean floor. The poop deck where the passengers and crew had finally gathered was obscured by a portion of the rear well deck that had been ripped up and folded over. There, on what little of the poop deck could be seen, Alvin hovered and dropped a small plaque in memory of the dead.

The expedition ended and they went back home with images that soon flooded onto television screens around the world. From these it became clear that the ship had suffered for her 73 years under water; some had hoped that the lack of oxygen at such a depth would have preserved her perfectly. However, small sea creatures and sea water had eaten into and dissolved the ship's ornate woodwork and nothing of an organic nature had survived:

no food, no clothes, no bodies and no bones, just occasionally a pair of shoes, the treated leather having discouraged any ravenous sea creatures, that showed where a body had once lain. The steel hull itself was a total wreck through its destruction and had been worn and pitted by the sea; where bacteria had been to work, fragile stalactites of rust hung around the frame of what in its heyday had been a ship of beauty.

These two expeditions brought nothing back from the wreck and its integrity was preserved. However, a year later, much to the disappointment of many, Dr. Ballard included, a separate expedition to the wreck returned with a selection of artefacts from the Titanic and, despite assurances that the wreck would not be damaged, some harm was done. The hope that the Titanic could be left undisturbed was shattered and many felt that a grave had been desecrated.

The greatest legacy for historians of the Titanic is that the expeditions to the ship cleared up old arguments and posed new, interesting questions. Positive proof can now be given that the Titanic had broken into two pieces as many witnesses testified and the long-held theory of the 300 feet long gash was questioned. Also, more contentious issues were dragged back into the public arena. The team found that the Titanic was some distance off from the estimated position given by Fourth Officer Boxhall, a fact that sparked a resurgence of the old controversy concerning the steamship Californian and the culpability of her commander. A fresh investigation was made of the evidence and gave judgement in 1992. To the disappointment of the Lordites, Captain Stanley Lord was again officially censured for ignoring the Titanic's distress rockets, though it was also noted that the Californian was too far away to have reached the Titanic in time.

But what about Smith? In Stoke-on-Trent, interest in Captain Smith was renewed through the two expeditions and the judgment, but so too were the old arguments as to how his actions or lack of action had contributed to the disaster. Calls were made for a statue of Smith to be erected in Hanley or at least for the one in Lichfield to be resited in the Potteries. Apparently, this last option was considered and a request was made to the Lichfield authorities for the statue there to be taken to Hanley. However, Lichfield turned down the request and refused to relinquish the statue that many of its inhabitants had once argued against so bitterly. The Stoke-on-Trent council did not pursue the matter after this, but instead considered their other option of having a new statue made especially for the town, although nothing has yet materialised.

Smith's epitaph seems to be "the man who sank the Titanic", but his part in the disaster that overtook the ship on that cold April night in 1912 was just one small piece in an unparalleled series of unlikely events, a jigsaw puzzle that unkind fate seems to have put together. For instance, Smith has always been accused of running his ship into the ice field against the usual wisdom in such matters, but this is essentially a view created with hindsight, bearing the lessons of the Titanic in mind. A standard reference book, "The Oxford Book Of The Sea", makes no bones about it – Smith was following standard procedure. In 1912, it was common practice, if visibility was good and the sea was calm, for liner captains to take their ships through ice fields at speed and a number of other experienced liner captains testified to this at the disaster inquiries. The British inquiry put this down to competition between shipping companies rather than to the whim of individual captains – a verdict that was probably fairly close to the mark.

Smith was not drunk in charge of his ship, nor, as others claim, was he hobnobbing with passengers when he should have been on the bridge; he had been in his sea cabin just behind the bridge since 9.20 p.m. and had asked to be kept informed. Also, the other senior officers were capable of command in their own right, some of them being qualified extra master mariners, and it was their duty to hold the watch in the captain's place. Had Smith been on the bridge at the time, given the amount of time between the warning and the collision, he could have done no more than was done by First Officer Murdoch. The lack of lifeboats aboard was not his fault and the inability to contact nearby ships was beyond his control.

The only charge that can be levelled at Smith in relation to the Titanic is one of overconfidence. He believed that the Olympic-class liners were in his words, 'firm as a church'– his own variation on the theme of the Titanic being unsinkable. During his long career, he had seen the demise of the sailing ship and watched with interest the rise of these powerful new steamers, which, with all their mod cons and turbine engines, were an age away from the ships in which he had first gone to sea. It may well be, as several authors have since suggested, that Smith, and by extension the entire generation of sailors then in service, had let the technology outgrow them. Perhaps Smith was still a small ship captain. Maybe his reasoning was that just as increased technology meant increased comfort, increased speed also meant increased safety. However, going twice as fast does not make things twice as safe, but twice as dangerous and a ship that doubles in size has its manoeuvrability cut in half. As was shown with the Olympic-Hawke incident and the Titanic's near accident with the New York, sailors still had a lot to learn about how to handle ships of the bulk of the Titanic.

Before encountering the iceberg, these lessons still had to be learned and a situation which could have been easily avoided in smaller ships, such as the Republic or Majestic, whose slower speeds and tighter turning circles allowed them to dodge icebergs, may have given Smith a false sense of safety – after all, he had safely negotiated ice fields in the past, so why not in the future? But he had never taken a ship of this size into an ice field before and though the manoeuvre executed before the iceberg at 500 yards would have saved a smaller, slower ship, it was not so with the Titanic, as she was too big and going too fast under the guidance of men still unsure as to the sheer raw kinetic energy such a vessel embodied. It was as classic a case of an irresistible force meeting an immovable object as could be imagined and was all caused by overconfidence. Yet, everything is relative and Smith and the officers who served under him were the products of an overconfident age, basking as they were in the wake of an industrial revolution and a golden age of empire on which the sun seemed unlikely to set. Without the lessons to show how lacking they were in knowledge or how wrong the assumptions were, overconfidence was a common fault. So is it only in the light of the disaster that occurred that some have judged Smith so harshly – did he alone cause the disaster? Or was it a fact that his faults were those of an entire people, an entire system and an entire age? Was he just a small cog in a very big and faulty machine?

Perhaps Smith should rather be judged by looking at his entire career. He was a man who mixed easily with millionaires and nobility, but he never forgot his old friends, nor was he ashamed of his roots, though his roots later seemed ashamed of him. He was regarded as a fair commander, a kindly man who ran a tight but happy ship. With his officers he was 'exceedingly popular' and crews enjoyed sailing under his command. Passengers chose to travel with Smith personally because of his affability, but also because, by the standards of the time, he was an excellent sailor who felt deeply the responsibility of command and who, when it came to the ultimate test of that responsibility, behaved very bravely, never once shirking his burden. To all of these people, passengers and crew, and especially to Herbert Lightoller, Smith was regarded as the best sea captain they had ever known. With hindsight, though it is easy, necessary even, to mock their nationalistic motives in praising the man, it is nonetheless still easy enough to imagine more human and personal reasons why many people would want to remember a man whom they had regarded as their friend.

In Stoke-on-Trent there are still people who do not want any notice paid to Smith, people who still feel troubled by the disaster. However, there are many who have cultivated something akin to a rough affection for this much maligned man, who rose from a working-class background, worked hard and carved himself a place in society – there is certainly nothing to be ashamed of in that. It is not, of course, that Smith hasn't earned himself a place in the local black humour. 'Be British!' has often been twitted and one good joke has his famous last words as being, 'Where's all this bloody water coming from?' But there is some affection there, even when he is merely remembered as 'the Hanley lad who sank the Titanic'.

As for the embarrassment that Smith is supposed to have caused the Potteries, with the passage of time this seems to have generally been eroded and, since the discovery of the Titanic, has mainly given way to a natural and perhaps long overdue interest in the man. The memorial plaque, which was held so long at the

Etruria Middle School, was resited in Hanley Town Hall in the late 1970s and now attracts a few more eyes than before. And in the new Potteries Shopping Centre in Hanley, a mural has been painted showing some of the local men and women who have made their mark in the world. Novelist Arnold Bennett glowers out from a scene of fiery pot banks and characters from his tales, footballer Stanley Matthews weaves his way around the opposition and with them on the stairs, next to Spitfire designer Reginald J. Mitchell, is Captain Smith in his white uniform, merging into the iceberg, towering over the angled stern of the doomed Titanic.

Even as the first edition of this book was being finished in 1992, the 80th anniversary of the sinking of the Titanic came and went, with the main item of interest being the findings of the fresh inquiry into the actions of Captain Lord. But Smith was again in the news, at least in north Staffordshire. On 15th April, the "Evening Sentinel" carried a large article on the disaster and the city's connection with it. A pottery firm turned out a limited edition of Captain Smith figurines and then there was a mild controversy over a junior chamber of commerce that had the Titanic as their theme for an annual dinner and said that "There'll Always Be An England" was sung as the ship went down, though this song originally came from the 1940 tub-thumping film "Discoveries"! More interesting was a display dedicated to Smith held in Stoke-on-Trent City Museum, the first time that it had featured an exhibition related to this otherwise forgotten son. It contained an assortment of objects connected to Smith, most notably a brass telescope and sextant that had belonged to him, and there were various papers and articles, most of which were on loan for the display.

So, at last, the Hanley lad who went to sea has finally come home. Smith has been and will perhaps always remain a rather troublesome son for the City of Stoke-on-Trent, even though he has at last gained the rather dubious status of a "local hero". Maybe that is how it should be. After all, the millionaires that knew him and the society that fêted him are dead and gone, so perhaps it is now the responsibility of the city that tried to forget him to remember Commander Edward John Smith R.D., R.N.R., whose image tide and time have reshaped, just as they have the wreck of the legendary Titanic.

Chronology Of Captain Smith And His Family

c. 1805	Edward Smith was born in Hanley.
1809	Catherine Marsh was born in either Stoke-upon-Trent or Penkhull.
13th June 1831	George John Hancock, potter, and Catherine Marsh were married in Wolstanton.
c. 1833	Joseph Hancock was born in Penkhull.
1st January 1836	Thirza Hancock was born in Wolstanton (or possibly Tunstall).
17th January 1836	Thirza Hancock was baptised at Tunstall Primitive Methodist Chapel.
1847	Edward Smith, potter, and Catherine Hancock were married in Wolstanton.
27th January 1850	Edward John Smith was born at 51 Well Street, Hanley.
30th March 1851	Census return showed four people living at 51 Well Street: Edward Smith, potter, 46; Catherine Smith, grocer, 42; Thirza Hancock, milliner and dressmaker, 16 (sic); Edward John Smith, infant, 1.
1851 or 1852	The family moved, taking over the grocer's store at 17 Well Street (comprising 'house, shop and yard' owned by Elizabeth Smith).

1852–53	Edward Smith was listed as a 'Shop-keeper' in the 1852-53 edition of "Slater's Commercial Directory".
c. 1853–62	Ted Smith attended the Etruria British School, Etruria.
c. 1862–67	Ted worked at Etruria Forge, for some time as the Nasmyth steam hammer operator.
February 1867	Ted went to Liverpool with a group of friends, one of whom was Joseph Turner.
5th February 1867	Ted was signed on as "boy" aboard the Liverpool-registered sailing ship, Senator Weber (or Senator Webber), commanded by his half-brother Joseph Hancock. Ted became an apprentice with the shippers Messrs. Andrew Gibson & Co. of Liverpool.
5th February 1867–8th February 1868	Ted served as boy aboard the Senator Weber.
9th February 1868–3rd September 1870	Ted served as the 3rd mate aboard the Senator Weber.
18th October 1870–6th March 1871	Ted worked as an able seaman aboard the Halifax, Nova Scotia-registered vessel, Amoy.
1871	The Smith family and shop moved to 30 Well Street, Hanley.
2nd April 1871	Joseph Hancock and Edward John Smith, both listed as seamen, were resident at 30 Well Street when the census was taken.
24th March–15th July 1871	Ted served as an able seaman aboard the Liverpool-registered sailing ship, Madge Wildfire.
21st July 1871	Ted applied for the examination for 2nd mate. His address was then the Sailors' Home, Liverpool.

24th July 1871	Ted passed the 2nd mate's exam. He received his certificate on 12th August 1871.
24th August 1871- 19th January 1872	Ted served as the 2nd mate aboard the Liverpool-registered ship, Record.
28th February- 27th July 1872	Ted served as the 2nd mate aboard the Windward Isles-registered ship, Agra.
27th September 1872 -3rd March 1873	Ted served as the 2nd mate aboard the Quebec-registered, N. Mosher.
22nd March 1873	Ted applied for the examination for 1st mate. His address was then 5 Hanover Street, Liverpool.
25th March 1873	Ted passed the 1st mate's exam. He received his certificate in Bremerhaven, Germany on 8th April.
15th July 1873- 4th May 1875	Ted served three terms aboard the Liverpool-registered ship, Arzilla, as the 1st mate.
19th May 1875	Ted applied for the examination for the master's ordinary certificate of competency.
22nd May 1875	Ted passed the master's exam. He received his certificate on 26th May 1875.
May 1876	Smith was given his first command, the 1,040 ton, full-rigged, Liverpool-registered sailing ship, Lizzie Fennell.
May 1876- January 1880	Smith commanded the Lizzie Fennell, which operated between Liverpool and South America.
March 1880	Smith joined the White Star Line.
March 1880- March 1882	Smith served as fourth and later third officer aboard the S.S. Celtic.
March 1882- March 1884	Smith served as second officer aboard the S.S. Coptic in the Pacific service.

March 1884- July 1885	Smith served as second officer aboard the S.S. Britannic.
July 1885- April 1887	Smith served as first officer aboard the S.S. Republic.
29th December 1885	Edward Smith died in Runcorn, Cheshire.
13th January 1887	Edward John Smith married Sarah Eleanor Pennington at St. Oswald's Church at Winwick, near Warrington.
April- August 1887	Smith assumed temporary command of the S.S. Republic.
August 1887- February 1888	Smith was transferred to the S.S. Britannic as her first officer.
1888	Smith joined the Royal Naval Reserve.
14th February 1888	Smith failed in his first attempt for his extra master mariner's certificate, losing out on the navigation section.
17th February 1888	Smith applied to take the exam again.
20th February 1888	Smith gained his extra master mariner's certificate.
April-May 1888	Smith commanded the S.S. Baltic, his first transatlantic command.
June-September 1888	Smith commanded the S.S. Britannic.
December 1888	Smith was given command of the cattle transporter, Cufic, and took the ship on her maiden voyage.
January 1889	Smith assumed full command of the S.S. Republic.
April-July 1889	Smith commanded the S.S. Celtic.
December 1889- December 1890	Smith commanded the S.S. Coptic in the Australian service.
December 1890- February 1891	Smith returned to the north Atlantic run as captain of the S.S. Adriatic.
March-April 1891	Smith commanded the S.S. Runic.

May 1891– May 1893	Smith returned as captain of the S.S. Britannic.
c. 1893	Joseph Hancock died of heart disease.
June 1893	Smith briefly commanded the S.S. Adriatic.
July 1893– January 1895	Smith was back in command of the S.S. Britannic.
1st November 1893	Catherine Smith died in Runcorn.
January 1895	Smith˙ briefly returned to command the S.S. Cufic.
January–April 1895	Smith returned for his final period in command of the S.S. Britannic.
May–June 1895	Smith commanded the S.S. Germanic.
July 1895– November 1902	Smith commanded the S.S. Majestic.
1899–1901	The S.S. Majestic, with Smith in command, made two trips to South Africa, with troops for the Boer War.
1902	Helen Melville Smith was born.
December 1902– May 1903	Smith commanded the S.S. Germanic, while the Majestic underwent alterations.
1903	King Edward VII presented Smith with the Transport Medal with the "South Africa" clasp for his Boer War service.
11th May 1903	Smith drew up his will, leaving all to his wife and daughter.
May 1903– June 1904	Smith returned as captain of the S.S. Majestic.
29th June 1904– March 1907	Smith commanded the new S.S. Baltic, the largest ship in the world at that time.
1907	Smith became a member of the executive council of the Mercantile Marine. White Star moved its transatlantic operations to Southampton. The Smiths took up

	residence at Woodhead, a house in Winn Road, Westwood Park, Southampton. Smith may for a short time have taken command of the S.S. Oceanic.
8th May 1907–February 1911	Smith commanded the new S.S. Adriatic.
1910	Smith was awarded the Royal Naval Reserve Long Service Medal and had the right to have the words 'Reserve Decoration' (i.e. 'R.D.') after his name.
May 1911–March 1912	Smith commanded the new R.M.S. Olympic, then the largest ship in the world. Her maiden voyage took place on 11th June 1911.
20th September 1911	The R.M.S. Olympic was involved in a collision with the Royal Navy cruiser H.M.S. Hawke.
1912	Commander Edward John Smith became Commodore of the White Star Line.
10th April 1912	The R.M.S. Titanic, under Smith's command, set out from Southampton on her maiden voyage.
11.40 p.m., 14th April 1912	The R.M.S. Titanic collided with an iceberg, which severely damaged the ship below the water line.
2.20 a.m., 15th April 1912	The R.M.S. Titanic sank, taking 1,522 people with her. Captain Smith went down with his ship.
16th April 1913	A memorial plaque to Smith was unveiled in Hanley.
22nd April 1913	A framed photograph of Smith was unveiled at the Etruria Board School.
29th July 1914	A statue of Smith, sculpted by Lady Kathleen Scott, was unveiled in Lichfield,

Staffordshire, by the captain's daughter, Helen.

28th April 1931	Eleanor Smith was killed in a road accident.
1972	Mrs. Simon Russell Cooke (née Helen Melville Smith) died.

Glossary

Aft: Towards the rear of a ship.

Astern: The same as aft, though the term can also be used in reference to a ship going in reverse, e.g. going astern.

Boat Deck: The deck on which a ship's lifeboats are carried, usually the uncovered upper deck on a ship's superstructure.

Bow: The pointed forward end of a ship.

Bridge: The command centre aboard a ship, usually a raised cabin, with wings stretching to either side of the ship – the "bridge" from which it gets its name. The bridge is essentially a watching post, which contained the main telegraphs at the time of the Titanic. The wheelhouse was usually situated just behind the main bridge during that period.

Bulkhead: A vertical partition of a ship's interior. Bulkheads are a standard feature in the construction of watertight compartments.

Capstan: Large copper or, more usually, bronze spindles fixed on the upper deck, used in the winding and unwinding of ropes, especially during docking.

CQD: The earliest form of wireless distress signal when using Morse code. "CQ" meant 'Attention all stations', while the "D" suffix classified it as a distress signal. The code was sent "tight" (i.e. without any long gaps) as a Morse code signal and the letters were used as they meant nothing other than a distress call when used in this manner. The signal was given the popular meaning of "Come Quick Danger". The signal was gradually replaced from 1908 by SOS.

GLOSSARY

Davits: Arm-like steel cranes arranged in pairs alongside a ship to carry and lower the lifeboats. The type carried on the Titanic were Welin davits which were particularly well-made items and were able to compensate for the slant that the Titanic developed.

Falls: The system of ropes by which lifeboats are lowered down to the sea.

Field Ice: As the name itself implies, field ice is an expanse of ice covering a wide area. Either formed of small broken lumps from icebergs or frozen sea water, field ice, though slight in the water and without the density or danger of Arctic pack ice, is still a considerable obstacle.

Forecastle or Fo'c'sle: The raised deck on the bow of a ship, where the ship's crew lived. The name dated back to the earliest wooden fighting ships where the foredeck was built up like a castle.

Foremast: The leading mast on a ship. The Titanic had a foremast and a mizzenmast, though neither was rigged for sail. The Titanic's foremast carried the ship's crow's-nest and a mast light, as well as supporting one end of the wireless aerial.

Forepeak: A watertight ballast tank in the very nose of a ship, which, with a similar tank in the stern, can be flooded or emptied to trim the ship in the water.

Forward: The front part of a ship, towards the bow.

Galley: A ship's kitchen.

Growlers: The smallest classification of iceberg.

"Hard-a-starboard" – Helm Orders: On the Titanic when the order rang out 'Hard-a-starboard', the ship turned to port. This was because the old form of helm orders was still in common usage. This was a throwback to the days when ships were steered by the tiller rather than the ship's wheel. The tiller bar was connected directly to the rudder, so if you wanted the craft to go to port you had to push the bar to starboard, hence "Hard-a-starboard". These old orders were somewhat confusing to newcomers, especially those brought into the service during World War One, and they became obsolete before World War Two.

Hull: The outer "skin" of a ship. Originally, clinker-built and later caulked wooden hulls formed the ship, but these gave way to steel plates over wood (ironclads) and finally to the all-metal hull formed from sheets of riveted plate steel.

Keel: The spine of a ship. The keel is formed by the main construction spar that runs down the middle of the ship's underside, though the term is also more generally applied to the whole of a ship's underside.

Knot: A nautical mile measuring 6,082 feet, as opposed to a land mile of 5,280 feet.

Mainmast: The main and usually middle mast on a sailing ship.

Mizzenmast: The rear mast on a sailing ship.

Morse Code: A system of communication developed by Samuel Morse, whereby letters of the alphabet, or single words and phrases, are represented as a series of electrical or light pulses in either short or long flashes ("dots" and "dashes"). For example, SOS is rendered as '... ___ ...'

Morse Lamp: A manually operated lamp used to signal in Morse code to nearby ships.

Poop Deck: The raised stern deck on a ship.

Port: The left-hand side of a ship, originally called larboard.

Prow: The leading edge of a ship's bow.

Quarter: The quarter represents the rear 90° on either side of a ship, what on land would be called either the right or left flank.

Reciprocating Engine: A ship's steam engine, operating on a principle similar to most forms of engine, with a piston and crank system. Steam was used to power a piston, the transferred energy from which was pushed through 90° via the crank and turned the propeller shaft. The Titanic's engines were the four-cylinder triple expansion type (sometimes called quadruple expansion because of the four cylinders). These reciprocating engines powered the two large wing propellers, one per propeller.

Rig: The term describing the set-up of masts and sails on a sailing ship. The type of rig determines how a ship is classified.

Rigging: The two kinds of rigging on a sailing ship are the standing rigging, including the rope ladders or "shrouds", which holds the mast in place or acts as support lines for crewmen when aloft, and the running rigging, which is used in trimming and positioning the sails.

R.M.S.: Royal Mail Ship or Royal Mail Steamer.

Sextant: A navigational instrument, whereby angles of celestial bodies to the earth can be calculated by a method of reflection, so allowing an estimation of a ship's relative position.

SOS: The standard international distress signal when using Morse code. It took the place of CQD from 1908, because if sent incorrectly, CQD was open to some misinterpretation. SOS was instantly recognisable as it had no other meanings beyond being a call for help. It has since been wrongly interpreted as meaning "Save Our Souls". Since the advent of radio communications, SOS has given way to the "Mayday" spoken distress call.

S.S.: Abbreviation of "Steam ship".

Starboard: The right-hand side of a ship.

Steerage: The old term for what in 1912 was officially third-class travel and accommodation. In the past, accommodation on ships was either first-class or steerage, though the gradual introduction of second-class altered this. Steerage was the cheapest rate of travel, chiefly given over to emigrants. On the Titanic, though the steerage accommodation was considered spartan in comparison to first-class, it was of a neat, utilitarian aspect that would not look out of place today.

Stern: The rear end of a ship.

Telegraph System: The ship's telegraph signalling system, principally between the main bridge and the engine room, was an electrically operated means of communication. The telegraph on the bridge was used to ring down to the engine room a particular command which was shown by a setting on the round engine room telegraph indicator. The positions on the indicator gave some latitude for speed from "Dead Slow" to "Slow", "Half" and "Full". There was a further set of commands for going astern. There were also telegraphs fitted on the docking bridge. On the Titanic, the docking bridge was a raised superstructure on the poop deck that was principally used during manoeuvres whilst in harbour.

Turbine Engine: The Titanic carried a single turbine engine which powered the smaller four-bladed central propeller. Working on a different principle to the reciprocating engines, this engine made use of steam from the low-pressure cylinders of the other engines, which was projected in a jet over a bladed rotor which span around. The energy from this was transferred through a system of gears to the central propeller shaft.

Well Decks: The sheltered decks between the forecastle and the poop deck and the ship's central superstructure. These usually housed the cargo hatches that reached down to the holds and the mail room.

Wheelhouse: A small cabin contained within the bridge of a ship, from where the ship was steered.

Bibliography

BALLARD, Dr. Robert D., "The Discovery of the Titanic", Hodder and Stoughton Ltd., London, 1987.

BEESLEY, Lawrence, "The Loss of the S.S. Titanic. Its Story and its Lessons", 7C's Press Inc., Riverside, Connecticut, U.S.A., 1973.

BEHE, George, "Titanic: Psychic Forewarnings of Disaster", Patrick Stephens Ltd., Wellingborough, 1988.

DAVIE, Michael, "The Titanic – The Full Story of a Tragedy", Grafton Books, London, 1987.

EATON, John P., & HAAS, Charles A., "Titanic – Triumph and Tragedy: A Chronicle in Words and Pictures", Patrick Stephens Ltd., Wellingborough, 1986.

EATON, John P., & HAAS, Charles A., "Falling Star – Misadventures of White Star Line Ships", Patrick Stephens Ltd., Wellingborough, 1989.

GRACIE, Colonel Archibald, "The Truth About the Titanic", 7C's Press Inc., Riverside, Connecticut, U.S.A., 1973.

HARRISON, Leslie, "A Titanic Myth: The Californian Incident", William Kimber & Co. Ltd., London, 1986.

JAMIESON, W.M., "Murders, Myths and Monuments in North Staffordshire", Westmid Supplies Ltd., Shrewsbury, 1979.

LIGHTOLLER, C.H., "Titanic and Other Ships", Withy Grove Press, London, 1939.

LORD, Walter, "A Night to Remember", Penguin Books Ltd., Middlesex, 1976.

LORD, Walter, "The Night Lives On", Viking-Penguin Books Ltd., Middlesex, 1986.

STUART, Denis, (Editor), "People of the Potteries", Keele University, Newcastle-under-Lyme, 1985.

BIBLIOGRAPHY

WARRILLOW, E.J.D., "A Sociological History of the City of Stoke-on-Trent", Etruscan Publications, Stoke-on-Trent, 1960.
WARRILLOW, E.J.D., "History of Etruria", Etruscan Publications, Stoke-on-Trent, 1953.
ADDITIONAL SOURCES: "Report on the Loss of the S.S. Titanic", British inquiry report, reprinted by Alan Sutton Publishing Ltd., Gloucester, 1990.
"Staffordshire Sentinel" and "Evening Sentinel", various issues.